Australian National Gallery

ISBN 0 642 88709 8

Print Department staff in the opening year

Cathy Clynes — *Curatorial Assistant*
Stephen Coppel — *Curatorial Assistant*
Pat Gilmour — *Senior Curator*
Sara Kelly — *Museum Assistant*
Margaret MacKean Taylor — *Visiting Curator*
Bernard McLindon — *Museum Assistant*
David Maybanks — *Museum Assistant*
Colleen Misson — *Secretary*
Tony Palmer — *Assistant Curator*
Kay Vernon — *Curatorial Assistant*
Jane White — *Curatorial Assistant*
Anne Willsford — *Curatorial Assistant*

Exhibitions staff who assisted with *Paperwork*: Rod Bolton, Gavan Desmond, Tony Leitch, Nat Williams

Photography: Bruce Moore, Gordon Petherbridge, Erwin Potas
Co-ordinator of Publications: Alan Dodge
Editor: Laura Murray
Typesetting: Smith & Miles Ltd, Sydney
Printing: Champion Press, Sydney
Designed by Alistair Hay

Paperwork

Written and researched by
Pat Gilmour and Anne Willsford

Australian National Gallery Canberra 1982.

As is the case in any undertaking, the Department of International Prints could not have completed its work without the assistance of all the other Departments within the Gallery, from Finance and Purchasing to Security and Office Services.

It has also enjoyed the advice and support of Daniel Thomas and Roger Butler from the Department of Australian Art and from the Gallery's Paper Conservator, Seumas Andrewartha.

But its greatest good fortune has been that its first Print Curator, Margaret MacKean Taylor, out of her abiding affection for the Gallery, returned to help us in this opening year. Her capacity for generating excitement and the exemplary standards that she has set will be an enduring inspiration.

Introduction

Traditionally, prints have been discussed in terms of three separate facets — their subject matter, the techniques used in their making and the background to the image, which has customarily been paper.

This background has been so invisible, that when in 1977 Andrew Robison mounted an exhibition called 'Paper in Prints' at the National Gallery of Art in Washington, it was the first systematic treatment of the subject ever.

Robison's exhibition was inspired by the remarkable interest that artists in the United States were by then taking in the actual act of papermaking. This reached a peak during the first half of the 1970s when, no longer merely the background to an image, paper became an independent means of expression often combining subject, process and support into a single entity.

In this catalogue we look at:

a) artists who have used traditional processes for embossing without ink in such a way that the paper becomes the image;
b) artists who, while still perceiving it essentially as a support, have either chosen an existing paper to reinforce meaning, or have had a special paper custom made;
c) artists who have burnt, folded, perforated or torn paper to make an image, with or without the addition of printing;
d) artists who have painted with pulp, by introducing dyes at the wet stage of papermaking or by laminating layers of coloured pulp together;
e) artists who have cast paper in three-dimensional reliefs or as editioned sculptures;
f) artists who have celebrated the intrinsic characteristics of paper, by recycling pulp or presenting the watermark as the image;
g) and one artist who humorously commented on the craze for working in pulp by screenprinting his 'hand-made' paper.

Footnote:
Artists whose names appear in bold in this catalogue are represented in the 'Paperwork' exhibition with works from the Australian National Gallery's collection of international prints.

A two-part bibliography is to be found at the end of this catalogue : the first part gives a list of general references; the second part, ordered under an alphabetical listing of artists represented in the exhibition, gives specific references for each artist.

Footnotes as such are not given. Quotations in the text are referenced in the bibliography by bracketed numbers in bold at the end of relevant book, journal or catalogue entries.

Embossing

Paper has been inklessly embossed to make an image for almost as long as prints have been made on it in the West. In the fifteenth century carved bone and ivory reliefs were imitated by the rare and very early 'seal prints' made by gently cajoling damp paper into the cuts in uninked wood blocks to create white embossing on white.

Woodblocks have therefore been used not only to print conventionally from inked shapes left in their surface by the cutter, but alternatively (or even simultaneously, as in the case of John Baptist Jackson, c1700-77) by creating three-dimensional bosses in the paper.

Jackson's combination of embossing with several colour blocks preceded by almost twenty years the polychrome printing of the famous Japanese Ukiyo-e ('transient world') school. By the 1790s, Japanese printers were able to register thirty colours perfectly in those prints which were to have such a dramatic effect in nineteenth century Europe on the development of the modern movement. At home they were considered cheap throwaway equivalents of Western fashion plates, postcard views or theatrical pin-ups, and they reached Europe in the mid-century when trade opened up with Japan, only because their soft paper made them ideal wrapping for porcelain exports.

Among the many refinements the Japanese employed was one called by the French 'gaufrage', (from gaufrer — to figure leather, flute linen, or corrugate paper). This inkless embossing or blind printing could convey the self-coloured textured weaves of richly patterned kimonos, the three-dimensional curve of a moon, or even a courtesan's cheek. Although the technique had been intermittently used in Europe since the fifteenth century, suddenly European artists, bowled over by Japanese art, discovered 'gaufrage' all over again.

Inspired by them, and in some cases using wood printed blind like the Japanese, later artists interested in embossing paper used some obscure and now discarded Victorian inventions such as the gypsograph (1837) and a variant, the glyphograph (1842). These developed from stereotyping, a means by which wood engravings intended to withstand long printing runs for periodicals, were moulded in plaster or papier maché then cast in type metal for greater durability. To adapt these replicating methods for printmaking, the artist worked into a layer of plaster (or similar white composition) spread on a metal plate darkened so he could see his progress. Then a metal relief printing block was cast in two stages from this three-dimensional drawing.

Maurice Dumont was a member of the generation of French Symbolist poets and artists who wanted art to become more spiritual in reaction to nineteenth century materialism and realism. Founder of an important avant-garde literary and artistic portfolio *L'Epreuve* (The Proof, 1894/95) which published prints by Gauguin, Vuillard and Bonnard, Dumont understood most graphic techniques. In 1895, when he was making a print for the first number of the German periodical *Pan*, he inked the uppermost part of his glyphograph with a single colour so that *Sappho*, a faintly medieval lady wandering in a flower-strewn wood, emerged both embossed and delicately outlined.

Artists who revived the art of the medal in the late nineteenth century saw the relationship between embossing paper and making low metal reliefs. Charpentier, perhaps France's most famous medallist, made moulds from layered cigarette papers for a whole range of embossed paper products, while **Pierre Roche**, fascinated by the mesmeric dancer Loie Fuller, sculpted her with the gypsograph. Loie Fuller, 'the electric fairy' who was also immortalized by Toulouse Lautrec, was the rage of Paris. She danced while multicoloured lights played on her iridescent veils. Her sinuous movements particularly delighted artists tending to exaggerate the expressive lines found in organic forms during the age of Art Nouveau.

Roche decorated the dancer's temporary theatre at the 1900 Paris Exhibition and four years later, illustrated the book about her by Roger-Marx. With their blue backgrounds, the sculptor's gypsographs resemble neo-classical figures on Wedgwood, heightened here and there with touches of brilliant colour.

Modelling paper to form an image was not confined to France. Japanese prints influenced **Koloman Moser**, who helped found the Vienna Secession in 1897 and the Vienna Werkstätte, an association of craftsmen, six years later. Moser was an Arts and Crafts professor noted for his pioneering abstract architectural ornament, his cleanly functional furniture and the flat stylization of his graphic designs for the Secession periodical, *Ver Sacrum*. His relief embossing of 1902, printed entirely without colour, betrays its debt to Japan by the way the figure is cut by the frame.

The twentieth century was well advanced before the sculptural manipulation of paper again became the concern of graphic artists, particularly those making intaglio prints between the wars.

The traditional relief print has ink applied to its surface and thence transferred to paper. The traditional intaglio etching or engraving, however, has its surface wiped and ink left primarily in the incisions the artist has made in the metal. As the plate passes through the press, its relatively uninked surface debosses a tell-tale indentation into the sheet, while the imagery cut into the metal is realized as a thread of ink on top of a cast of damp paper which heavy pressure has forced into the grooves.

The great discovery made by intaglio artists at this time was that it was possible to print surface and indentation simultaneously, not simply by leaving a fine film of ink on the plate (a common-place of intaglio printing), but by etching into or even through the plate, as well as building it up. In other words, the essentially three-dimensional nature of intaglio was freshly perceived.

The literal breakthrough came in 1925, when Rolf Nesch, a German refugee artist in Norway, accidentally etched a hole and discovered that when he printed the plate, his damp paper was formed into a raised bubble by it. Nesch not only made immediate use of this discovery for modelling a brick wall three-dimensionally and making the crystals of a glass chandelier stand out in relief, but began building up etched plates with soldered wires and ready-made meshes which could be embossed into a heavy paper. This activity gave birth to a new kind of print in the 1950s which the Americans called a collagraph.

A few years after Nesch, at the famous Parisian collaborative workshop, Atelier 17 that he founded, **S.W. Hayter** made related discoveries. Hayter, one of the most influential graphic artists of the twentieth century, whose workshop still serves famous artists and poor students alike, has played a crucial role in establishing printmaking as a major rather than subsidiary art form. Associated with the Surrealists, Hayter's automatic drawing took the form of engraved arabesques creating a kind of counterpoint between actual and illusory space, an option that the move away from traditional perspective and towards abstraction had increased. Noticing certain features of Japanese prints once again, Hayter realized that he could extend the relief of his work by creating deep uninked hollows or drilling holes through his plates. From 1933 to 1934, projecting bosses, giving the illusion of being even whiter than the rest of the paper, are frequently found in his prints. After the Second World War, they recur within complex compositions employing several inks deposited at different levels in the plate and printed simultaneously, a technical coup perfected in *Cinq personnages*.

One can see Hayter's influence everywhere, even in works totally unlike his own. The sculptor, Etienne Hajdu, working at Atelier 17 in 1957, was one of the first to revive a white on white image by embossing cut zinc shapes into paper.

Artists as far afield as the Columbian, Omar Rayo and the Yugoslav, Marjan Pogačnik, followed suit. The Swedish artist, **Birgit Skiold**, not only eventually applied Hayter's discovery to the inventive intaglio printing of lino, particularly appropriate for her book on the raked earth gardens of Kyoto, but in London, her adopted home, she set up England's first collaborative printmaking workshop based loosely on the Hayter model. Sadly, the artist died earlier this year before a book on papermaking, which she co-authored, was published.

Like Birgit Skiold, many artists have combined vestiges of colour with embossing. During the 1950s however, interest in the abstract manipulation of space through the relationship between the figure and the ground of an image, a new concentration on light as subject, and the use of monochrome in paintings by Yves Klein and Piero Manzoni, were all factors contributing to the fascination of embossing entirely without ink. Part of this movement, **Gunther Uecker**, kinetic artist of the German Zero group, developed all-over nail reliefs from 1957, intending them to appear dematerialized by light: inkless embossing translated this idea into print. **Helène Valentin**, whose paintings suggest space through colour, has embossed the same deep-cut plate into black, white, and cream sheets of hand-made paper.

Contemporary Japanese artists have also capitalized on the technical devices of their ancestors. **Hideo Hagiwara**, an innovator who has even printed splintery intaglio lines from wood, totally transforms his paper by working from both sides. Sometimes he forces pigment through the sheet from the back by placing it over an inked virgin block and burnishing it. In a print from his series on the martial arts, the paper was additionally embossed, until its other surface, coloured by a pale ink sparkling with mica dust, became a visual metaphor for armour.

Since the war, some of America's best-known artists have used inkless embossing. **Jasper Johns**, a key figure linking Abstract Expressionism to Pop Art and famous for painting everyday images such as flags and numerals, embossed the superimposed outlines of every letter of the alphabet into one sheet. Printed in a hydraulic forming press, the paper was sandwiched between positive and negative metal plates photoengraved from his drawing. A similar printing method was adopted for **Josef Albers**, whose wife, the weaver, **Anni Albers**, has also made embossed prints. Albers was a master at the famous German design school, the Bauhaus. He worked there until Hitler's closure of the school forced him to go to the United States to continue his teaching. An important influence in America both on optical art and the idea of painting in series, Albers had been among the earlier revivers of inkless embossing. Between 1958 and 1962 in his *Solo* and *Duo* suites featuring perceptually ambiguous forms, he explored imagery of a kind which recurs in his *Embossed linear constructions*.

Albers is famous for extending into printmaking the Bauhaus aesthetic that the hand made is not necessarily better than the machine made. By 1969 the traditional etching techniques he had previously used were superceded. Instead, his precision drawings were translated by an engineering programmer onto digital tape able to direct an automatic engraving mill to cut their mirror image into the printing plates. Of Albers' prints, Sheldon Nodelman observed, in a truism applying to most inkless embossing:

"The line is no longer imposed upon the surface but is drawn out of its very substance...The radiant whiteness of the paper, its finely woven texture, are no longer to be ignored as accidental features of an indifferent ground; they are now essential aspects of the total image.[1]"

Maurice Dumont
France 1870-1899
Sappho. 1895
colour glyphograph published in
Pan vol.I, no.1
28.0 x 36.4cm
unsigned, undated
purchased 1980
accession no. 1980.2811

Pierre Roche
France 1855-1922
La Loie Fuller by C. Roger-Marx
published Paris, Evreux, 1904
edition 71/130
illustrated by 17 colour gypsographs
page size 26.2 x 21.2cm
purchased 1980

Koloman Moser
Austria 1868-1918
The girl with long hair. 1902
inkless relief print
25.6 x 24.0cm
unsigned, artist's monogram,
undated, unnumbered
purchased 1980
accession no. 1980.2845

Stanley William Hayter
Great Britain/United States/France born 1901
Cinq personnages. 1946
burin and soft-ground etching printed
with 4 colours simultaneously on
Japanese Kochi paper
47.0 x 64.8cm
trial proof, signed, dated, titled,
numbered E 1/5 (edition 50)
purchased 1981
accession no. 1981.1809

Winged figures. 1952
burin engraving and soft-ground etching
66.8 x 52.0cm
signed, dated, numbered 88/90
published by Gutekunst and Klipstein, Berne
purchased 1979

Birgit Skiold
Sweden/Great Britain 1923-1982
Sound of one hand clapping. c1970
inkless embossing from gouged lino
with surface colour
52.5 x 36.0cm
signed, titled, numbered 4/25
purchased 1978

Zen gardens, 7 poems by James Kirkup
published by Circle Press, Guildford, 1973
illustrated by 7 photo-etchings with embossing
from lino
page size 29.7cm square
colophon page signed, numbered 51/100
purchased 1978

Gunther Uecker
West Germany born 1930
Untitled. 1971
inkless embossing
59.9 x 50.1cm
signed, dated, numbered 4/150
gift of Garry Anderson 1977

Helène Valentin
France/United States
Untitled. 1977
inkless embossing on cream
paper 70.5 x 50.8cm
artist's proof, signed on verso
gift of Garry Anderson 1977

Hagiwara, Hideo
Japan born 1913, Kofu
Man in Armor no.6. 1962
burnished woodcut with embossing, worked
from both sides of the Torinoko paper
99.2 x 66.0cm
signed, dated, titled, numbered 14/30
purchased 1973

Jasper Johns
United States born 1930, Georgia
Embossed alphabet. 1969
inkless embossing
75.5 x 94.5cm
signed, dated, inscribed 'RTP' (edition 70)
(Field 116)
published by Gemini G.E.L., Los Angeles
purchased 1974

Josef Albers
West Germany/United States 1888-1976
Embossed linear constructions. 1969
series of 8 inkless embossings
51.2 x 66.3cm
monogrammed, dated, numbered, each
inscribed 'ELC Right to print' (edition 100)
published by Gemini G.E.L., Los Angeles
purchased 1973

Anni Albers
West Germany/United States born 1899
Mountainous I-VI. 1978
6 inkless embossings from etched plates
each 56.2 x 52.7cm
signed, dated, numbered 'I to VI RTP'
respectively (edition 20)
published by Tyler Graphics Ltd, Bedford
Village, New York
purchased 1979
accession nos 1979.2921 to 2926

Pierre Roche
Illustration from *La Loie Fuller* by
C. Roger-Marx. 1904
colour gypsograph
page size 26.2 x 21.2cm

Pierre Roche
Illustration from *La Loie Fuller* by
C. Roger-Marx. 1904
colour gypsograph
page size 26.2 x 21.2cm

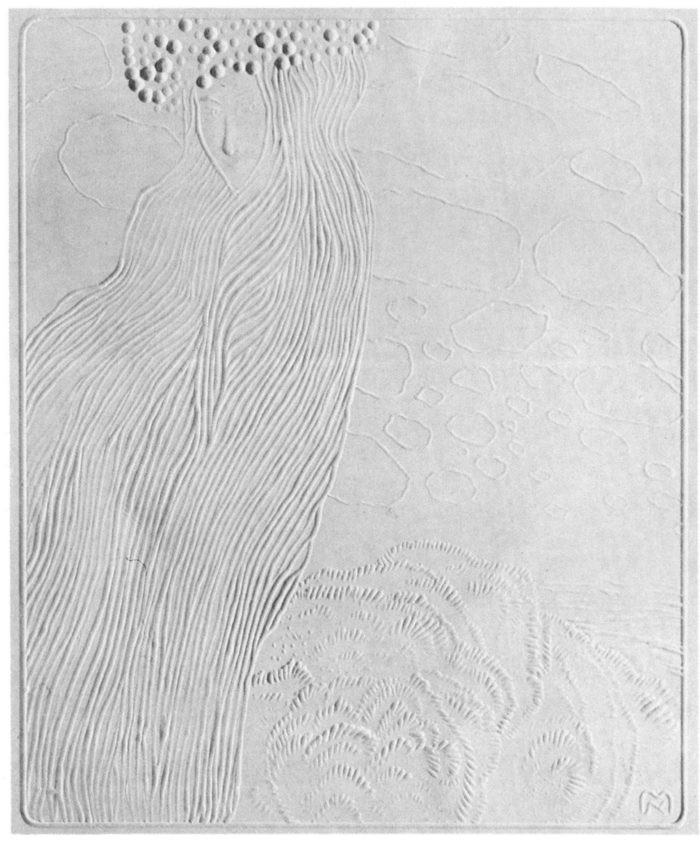

Koloman Moser
The girl with long hair. 1902
inkless relief print
25.6 x 24.0cm

Stanley William Hayter
Cinq personnages. 1946
burin and soft-ground etching printed with 4
colours simultaneously on
Japanese Kochi paper
47.0 x 64.8cm

Birgit Skiold
Sound of one hand clapping. c1970
inkless embossing from gouged lino with
surface colour
52.5 x 36.0cm

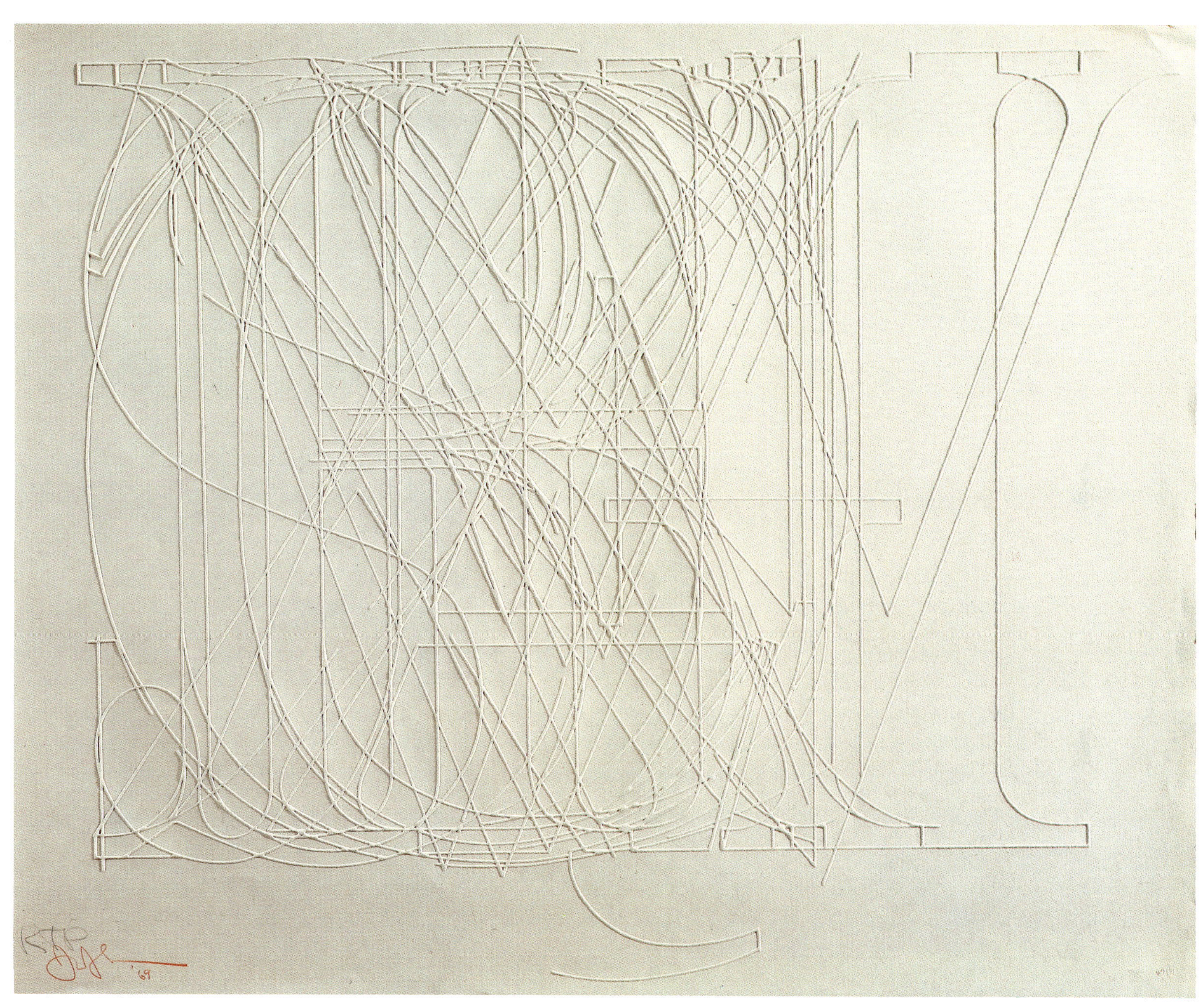

Jasper Johns
Embossed alphabet. 1969
inkless embossing
75.5 x 94.5cm

Anni Albers
Mountainous I. 1978
inkless embossing from etched plate
56.2 x 52.7cm

Anni Albers
Mountainous IV. 1978
inkless embossing from etched plate
56.2 x 52.7cm

Of course, artists must always have been aware of paper, even if mainly as a given, pre-existing surface. Robison makes a theoretic but convincing case that in the seventeenth century Rembrandt chose his printing surface for its receptivity to the etched cross-hatching so vital to his depiction of light, while Claude's buff papers intensified warm idylls in the Roman countryside. By the nineteenth century, there was an increasing incidence of coloured sheets to choose from: tan in Corot, light green for Meryon, orange for **The Douanier Rousseau's** *War*, and a startling yellow in **Paul Gauguin's** 1889 lithographs. Blue, one of the longest established paper colours, was employed in a lithotint *Nocturne* by Whistler, for whom the appropriation of various papers, which he often tore out of old books, was almost a fetish. Like an object lesson in Impressionism or Pointillism there was even a paper coloured with tiny red and blue rag flecks, which Camille Pissarro used in one of his lithographs.

Some artists have used readymade patterned papers. **Andy Warhol's** photo-screenprint of Merce Cunningham utilizes gaily patterned floral gift wrapping to convey the dancer's aesthetic. Over the years, Cunningham, with his musical director John Cage, has worked with a number of American artists in New York who have found in his pursuit of dance movement for its own sake, echoes of their non-referential painting. In 1954, Cunningham began a long association with the painter, Robert Rauschenberg, who was asked to make something the company 'could use in a dance'.

Since then, the troupe have performed against Stella's canvas strips, a set by Jasper Johns based on Duchamp's *Large glass*, Robert Morris' columns of light, Bruce Nauman's phalanx of electric fans, and Warhol's floating silver pillows. Warhol's screenprint was included in a portfolio by the seven artists most closely associated with the group, his patterned paper suggesting projected light and the aformal dancing without narrative or focus for which Merce Cunningham is famous.

Chine collé, in which a fine Oriental paper is adhered to a stronger sheet during the process of printing, is a device long used by artists. Whistler, for example, applied a fine warm straw colour in the area of the etched plate to the white sheets of his *French set*. More recently the Australian, **George Baldessin**, who died tragically in 1978, used aluminium foil in a similar way. When artists draw on metal to make an intaglio print, they have to imagine the effect when it is transposed to paper. By printing on foil, Baldessin carried over into the print the aesthetic effect apparent on his zinc plate.

Joe Tilson signalled a complete change of heart and philosophy by a change in the nature of process and material. One of the British 'Pop' generation, his work in the sixties was urban, political and technologically optimistic. Vacuum forming, backgrounds such as PVC and metallized acetates, were common in his work. By 1970, after a move to the country and deepening ecological concern, Tilson revised many of his stategies and began a body of prints, paintings and sculptures under the title *Alchera*, which derives from Australian Aboriginal dreamtime. Looking at ways in which primitive people structured their universe and exploring links between their cultures and his own, Tilson took the four elements as one of his themes, using beautiful hand-made Japanese papers and delighting in the meaning the sheets already possessed before he started work on them.

Inlaid beige chevrons in the brown sheet for *Earth* suggest ploughing, while pearlized whirls create a damask patterning in the white sheet for *Air*. Both prints consist of diverse images brought together in poetic association. In *Earth* these range from the Platonic solid with which the Greeks believed the element was constructed, to a tissue butterfly symbolizing seasonal rebirth, mandrakes thought in the Middle Ages to resemble people and to shriek when uprooted, reproductions of worm casts, a coarse tactile piece of mud-coloured paper and a spade the Tilsons bought in Italy, which they later discovered had remained unchanged since the fifteenth century when Piero della Francesca pictured it in his Arezzo frescoes.

Those of Tilson's screenprints previously printed on paper at Chris Prater's Kelpra Studio in London, had invariably been on either Arches or Rives BFK, both stable and dependable mouldmade papers from Europe providing a neutral, unobtrusive, yet high-quality background. Such papers are used for art because cheap paper degrades and falls to pieces, while good papers, if they are treated well, last indefinitely. Arches and Rives were precisely the papers that Ken Tyler, the master printer who in 1965 founded Gemini, a studio on America's West Coast, also used most consistently at the time. For since there were virtually no suitable papers for artists in general supply in the United States, all had to be imported.

Europe has enjoyed an unbroken tradition of printers and papermakers serving artists. At the beginning of the twentieth century, the great publisher, Vollard, for example, was able to command custom-made papers individually watermarked for his various enterprises. His favourite was the Montval paper developed by the sculptor Maillol and made by Canson and Montgolfier.

Tatyana Grosman, who began another famous printing and publishing studio called Universal Limited Art Editions on Long Island to persuade leading painters to make lithographs, was of Russian extraction. She had come to America from France however, and was therefore familiar with the European tradition. During the first few years that he worked at her shop, Jasper Johns used a different paper for practically every edition. It was Johns who, when he went to the American West Coast to work at Gemini in the second half of the 1960s, showed Tyler a hand-made paper that Fred Siegenthaler had sent him from Switzerland. But even then, it was for proofs rather than regular editions that Gemini experimented with such papers. In 1978 at the International Paper Conference in San Francisco, Tyler said that of 700 editions pulled during thirteen years' work, only 170 had been on hand-made sheets although by the time he spoke, the majority he worked with were custom made, sometimes by himself.

In the early days of his operation at Gemini, Tyler's quest for paper grew out of the conviction that really important prints would need to approach the scale of contemporary American painting to be taken seriously. This set in train a major research programme to find papers of sufficiently large scale to print **Robert Rauschenberg's** man-high *Booster* of 1967 incorporating the artist's own X-ray photographs. Tyler also wanted papers able to cope with particular printing problems, such as deep embossing. Within American industry, which was where his hopes began, such projects promised insufficient commercial return to warrant production. So Tyler approached a number of European paper mills. One of the lovely stories of this time relates how he demanded a whiter-than-white paper he saw at one mill, only to be told he would have to wait until February, when the frozen ground released less silt into the water. Amusingly enough, in negotiations with Arjomari Prioux at Epinal in France, Tyler requested paper produced in rolls which he would then cut to length. Such was the tradition of separately formed deckle-edged sheets in hand-made papers, however, that the firm refused to admit it had long been producing mouldmade continuous rolls and then hand tearing sheets with wooden slitters to simulate deckle!!

This problem resolved, Rauschenberg was able to produce on 'Special Arjomari' two of the largest hand-pulled lithographs ever made. *Sky garden* and *Waves*, each 225.5cm (89 inches) high, were part of the *Stoned moon* series of 1969 in which the artist celebated man's arrival on the moon.

In 1970, after five years of focusing his work on problems in "a world risking annihilation for the sake of a buck", Rauschenberg was filled with a desire to use everyday waste in some works the only message of which would be "a collection of lines imprinted like a friendly joke".[2] This time, Tyler developed a plastic-impregnated corrugated paper to make facsimiles of the dismembered cardboard boxes from which Rauschenberg fashioned several collage prints and a full scale double-sided *Cardbird door*.

Another source of paper for artists was however developing independently, from craft traditions. Dissatisfaction with standardization as a levelling-down process had produced craftsmen like the grand old man of American papermaking, Douglass Morse Howell. In his time, Howell has made special papers for artists as illustrious as Jackson Pollock. It was only when the printmaking 'renaissance' of the 1960s became so widespread that the kind of fine handmade paper he represented was needed in greater quantity.

Howell's most influential pupil was Laurence Barker, who, as head of printmaking at Cranbrook Academy, Michigan, started the first university paper mill in 1963. Directly or at one remove, Barker as teacher lies behind the majority of paper-makers who have proliferated all over the United States in the last decade; he himself now works in Barcelona.

In 1970, as he was preparing to leave the States for Spain, Barker met Tyler who had come to Cranbrook to conduct a printing workshop. Enthusiastic about the paper he saw there, Tyler asked Barker to make him some for use at Gemini. As he was so busy packing, Barker asked his graduate assistant, John Koller, to form the sheets. They were used for **Roy Lichtenstein's** handsome zinc line-cut of a 1930s-style head-form with overtones of Jawlensky's Constructivism. This was printed in black from the surface of the metal with the cut outline raising an uninked embossing in the sheet. Another print in the series employed die-cut white card over a dark embossed graphite composition.

Three years after their first meeting, Tyler rang Barker in Spain to ask for more paper to use at Gemini, but by the time Barker delivered the large delicate grey sheets requested, Tyler had left his partners to set up his own printing and publishing establishment on the East Coast of America, selling his collection of Gemini proofs to the Australian National Gallery.

Gemini used Barker's sheets for *Four Panels from 'Untitled 1972'* by **Jasper Johns**, a set of prints based on a unique work with disturbing and disjunctive imagery to which Johns has returned again and again. The left-hand sheet recalls decorative painting on an oncoming car glimpsed briefly one summer on Long Island. The two central sheets recreate fictive flagstones that Johns saw painted on a wall in Harlem, while the fourth pictures fragmented body parts from various of the artist's friends that appeared in the original work as wax casts. Concerned with perception and memory, the prints lie at the end of a long chain of analytical replication. They also encapsulate Johns' artistic repertoire moving from abstraction to realism, from flatness to illusory depth and from gestural mark to photo-reproduction.

After colour printing the first set on Barker's paper, Johns inklessly embossed the images from each of the four sheets into its neighbouring print on the right, to deny the drawing and increase the perceptual ambiguity. Concurrently between 1973 and 1975, Johns created a second set of prints using only grey and black inks on a more dominating grey paper with granular texture and highly irregular deckle, this time made by John Koller. Several of the original printing plates were reused, but taking the four panels as a whole, space and illusion were reduced, drawing strengthened, embossing omitted. Still haunting him, fragments of the same images were revived again in *Foirades/Fizzles* - Johns' intaglio embellishments for essays by Samuel Beckett on the impossibility of knowing oneself.

Before leaving for the East Coast of America in 1973, Tyler had not only engaged in a papermaking project at the pulp stage with Rauschenberg, but increasingly interested in special papers, had printed the *Soot-black stone* images for **Motherwell** on Hawthorne of Larroque hand-made paper from France, specially watermarked with the artist's initials. His new Bedford Village establishment was not far from Motherwell's studio, so Tyler was ideally placed to continue working with one of the few members of the Abstract-Expressionist generation to engage extensively in graphics. Inspired in the 1940s by Surrealist automatism and an interest in the unconscious as a force, Motherwell has been said to wield his brush like a Japanese killer. This appropriately describes the way he executes his lithographic ideographs direct onto the stone. *The stoneness of the stone* was "so essentially locked into that scale and into the colour of that stone", that Tyler asked the Twinrockers of Indiana (a second generation of hand papermakers) to laminate a pale grey sheet the colour of the stone onto a larger darker sheet of grey, providing a ground visually related to the print's making — a far cry from the bland and self-effacing papers of the 1960s.[3]

Custom-made papers and papers with meaning

Paul Gauguin
France 1848-1903
Bretonnes à la barrière (Breton women at the gate). 1889
lithograph on 'papier canari' (yellow paper)
50.0 x 34.8cm
signed in the plate, undated
(Guérin 4)
purchased 1972

The Douanier Rousseau
France 1844-1910
War. 1895
lithograph on orange paper
26.2 x 41.5cm
initialled in the plate, undated
purchased 1976

Andy Warhol
United States born 1928, Pittsburgh
Merce from *Merce Cunningham* portfolio 1974/75
screenprint on patterned paper
76.2 x 50.8cm
signed, numbered 28/100 on verso
published by Multiples Inc. and Castelli Graphics, New York
purchased 1979
accession no. 1980.779.07

George Baldessin
Australia 1939-1978
Pears (silver version). 1970
etching, aquatint on aluminium foil appliqué
signed, dated, titled, inscribed 'edition 25'
58.4cm square
gift of the artist, 1975

Joe Tilson
Great Britain born 1928, Sydenham
Earth and Air from the *Alcheringa* series. 1972
screenprint and collage on oriental paper
each 98.2 x 67.5cm
signed, dated and inscribed 'Artists proof' and 'A/P' respectively (editions 70)
published by Marlborough Graphics Ltd, London
purchased 1978

Robert Rauschenberg
United States born 1925, Texas
Cardbird door from *Cardbirds*. 1971
collage multiple imitating printed corrugated cardboard
204.0 x 95.0 x 32.5cm
signed, dated, numbered 25/25
published by Gemini G.E.L., Los Angeles
purchased 1975

Booster from *Booster and seven studies*. 1967
lithograph and screenprint
183.0 x 89.0cm
signed, dated, inscribed 'RTP' (edition 38)
published by Gemini G.E.L., Los Angeles
purchased 1973

Waves from *Stoned moon* series. 1969
lithograph on special Arjomari paper (edition 27)
226.0 x 107.0cm
signed, dated, inscribed 'RTP'
published by Gemini G.E.L., Los Angeles
purchased 1973

Roy Lichtenstein
United States born 1923, New York City
Modern head #3. 1970
from *Modern head* series
linecut and embossing from zinc plate on hand-made waterleaf paper
62.0 x 47.0cm

Modern head #5. 1970
from *Modern head* series
die-cut paper over embossed graphite composition
71.0 x 49.6cm
both signed, inscribed 'RTP' (editions 100)
both published by Gemini G.E.L., Los Angeles
purchased 1973

Jasper Johns
United States born 1930, Georgia
Four panels from 'Untitled 1972'. 1973/74
colour lithograph with embossing on pale grey hand-made Laurence Barker paper
four sheets — AD (Hatchings), BD and CD (Flagstones) and DD (Casts)
each 103.5 x 74.0cm irreg.
each signed, lettered, numbered AP IV/X, AD dated '73-'75 (edition 45)

Four panels from 'Untitled 1972' (grays and black). 1973/75
lithograph on dark grey hand-made John Koller paper
four sheets, each approx. 105.0 x 81.0cm
each signed, lettered, numbered AP 4/7, AD dated '73-'75 (edition 20)
(Field 194-197 and 198-201)
both sets published Gemini G.E.L., Los Angeles
purchased 1977

Robert Motherwell
United States born 1915, Washington
The stoneness of the stone. 1974
lithograph on two-tone grey laminated Twinrocker hand-made paper
105.5 x 77.6cm
signed, dated, inscribed 'OK to print.' (edition 75)
(Belknap 136)
published Brooke Alexander Inc., New York
purchased 1975

Paul Gauguin
Breton women at the gate. 1889
lithograph on yellow paper
50.0 x 34.8cm

The Douanier Rousseau
War. 1895
lithograph on orange paper
26.2 x 41.5 cm

Andy Warhol
Merce. 1974/75
from *Merce Cunningham* portfolio
screenprint on patterned paper
76.2 x 50.8cm

Robert Rauschenberg
Cardbird door. 1971
from *Cardbirds*
collage multiple imitating printed corrugated cardboard
204.0 x 95.0 x 32.5cm

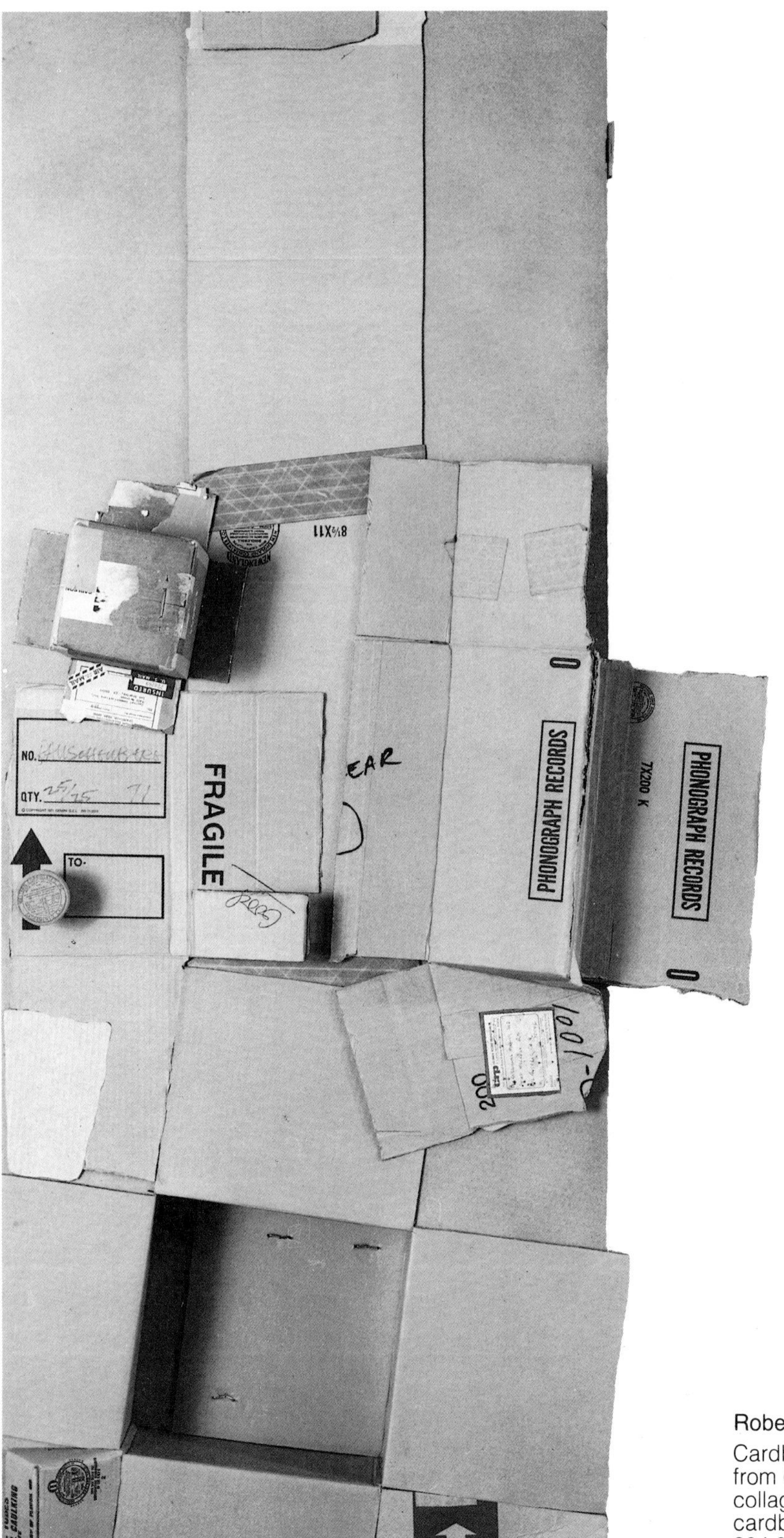

Robert Rauschenberg

Cardbird door. 1971
from *Cardbirds*
collage multiple imitating printed corrugated cardboard
204.0 x 95.0 x 32.5 cm

Joe Tilson
Earth. 1972
from *Alcheringa* series
screenprint and collage on oriental paper
98.2 x 67.5cm

Robert Rauschenberg
Booster. 1967
from *Booster and seven studies*
lithograph and screenprint
183.0 x 89.0cm

Robert Rauschenberg
Waves. 1969
from *Stoned moon* series
lithograph on special Arjomari paper
226.0 x 107.0cm

Roy Lichtenstein
Modern head #3. 1970
from *Modern head* series
linecut and embossing from zinc plate on hand-made waterleaf paper
62.0 x 47.0cm

Roy Lichtenstein
Modern head #5. 1970
from *Modern head* series
die-cut paper over embossed graphite composition
71.0 x 49.6cm

Jasper Johns
Panel A/D from *Four panels from 'Untitled 1972,* 1973/74
colour lithograph with embossing on pale grey hand-made Laurence Barker paper
103.5 x 74.0cm

Jasper Johns
Panel A/D, from *Four panels from 'Untitled 1972' (grays and black).* 1973/75
lithograph on dark grey hand-made John Koller paper
105.0 x 81.0cm

Jasper Johns
Panel D/D, from *Four panels from 'Untitled 1972.'* 1973/74
colour lithograph with embossing on pale grey hand-made Laurence Barker paper
103.5 x 74.0cm

Jasper Johns
Panel D/D, from *Four panels from 'Untitled 1972' (grays and black).* 1973/75
lithograph on dark grey hand-made John Koller paper
105.0 x 81.0cm

Robert Motherwell
The stoneness of the stone. 1974
lithograph on two-tone grey
laminated Twinrocker
hand-made paper
105.5 x 77.6cm

Although there are historical examples of many other kinds of usage, such as Japanese origami, paper has primarily been a surface for recording information. As Steven Kasher wrote in a recent article: "It exists to be obscured and aspires to whiteness only in order to make its obscuring more poignant".[4]

In the preliminary courses at the Bauhaus in the 1920s (which Josef Albers helped to devise) students were given projects intended to reveal new possibilities for paper. Its most familiar uses — as a flat sheet, or pasted for collage — were banned. Instead it had to be built as a construction, folded, employed with awareness of both its sides or its edge, and joined by unusual methods such as pinning and sewing. In the current emphasis on process and material, such possibilities have been taken up again by contemporary artists.

A remarkable symbiosis has sometimes been demonstrated between printing and painting. Richard Smith, for example, who was cutting and folding prints from 1968, got so interested in paper that he treated several canvases like sheets with turned-back corners. **Dorothea Rockburne** uses paper for most of her output, liking its impermanence. She chooses the plainest examples possible through which to realize works informed by principles of mathematical proportion, such as the golden section.

In her *Locus* series of folded prints, the method used in making them becomes the image, for idea, object and working procedure are inseparable. Guidelines etched faintly in grey on sheets of heavy white paper indicated the first fold to the artist, each subsequent fold being dictated by the previous one. Eventually the folded sheet, like a stage in origami, was printed from the relief surface of an aquatint plate inked in titanium white. The compression of the folded layers in the press created additional linear indentations; all help to form the image when the sheet is unfolded for display.

The Australian, **Robert Jacks**, has worked on a large scale. His heavy sculptural sheet of paper was cut in such a way that systematically modified tongues of the paper have curled out into three dimensions. This was part of a series of explorations by the artist which included other materials such as rubber and cloth.

Jay McCafferty has used the sun to make his works. In a ritualistic technique which results in the partial destruction of his materials, the artist directs the sun's rays with a magnifying glass in order to burn holes as indicated by a pencilled grid on stacked sheets of paper. These penetrating and charring solar burns expose successive layers of paper previously inked in bright colours by the artist.

Caroline Greenwald is interested in the Shinto philosophy of achieving oneness with nature by attempting to distil its essence. She is fascinated by change and variability in natural phenomena — clouds moving, snow falling, or waves frothing along the California coastline. While early works involved printing both sides of translucent paper and suspending it environmentally in space, she later became unwilling to impose an alien image on her materials. Now her more intimate and delicate paperworks take the form of folding maps or book and leaflet forms which can be tucked away in the envelopes she makes for them from traditional Mexican papers.

Sometimes drawing into damp paper with water, she combines and contrasts areas of heavier Western pulps with translucent Oriental papers. Lacy apertures, folds, puffs and pockets are combined with linear traceries of white animal hair, raw silk, or other vegetable fibres.

Like the artist Bill Weege of the Jones Road Print Shop and Stable in Wisconsin, with whom he has frequently collaborated, **Alan Shields** rejects most conventions, attempting to redefine and reinvent print processes. His prints may be cut, flocked, sewn or perforated and he has even woven sliced prints three-dimensionally, first printing the papers with every conceivable combination of techniques. The main printing device for the three circular *TV rerun* prints, was a hard rubber block incised with multiple grooves which the artist inked with many colours, then embossed into the sheets. Subsequently one disc had an added silver border, another was stamped by pencil eraser, while various intaglio printings and punched perforations were also employed.

His three square *Color radar smiles* were intended to be viewed on both sides. Openwork perforated sheets made of multicoloured papers laminated together at the wet stage were printed with both relief and intaglio processes.

A set of three-dimensional multiples made with Tyler in 1978 employed sheets of cream and grey fused together. After screen and lithographic printings, the paper was cut into five-centimetre strips, the edges stamped, and the strips slotted into interlocking grids. One set made a loose weave square, another a diamond, while the third was slung like a hammock in a pyramidal perspex box.

Folding/Burning/Perforating/Tearing

Dorothea Rockburne
Canada/United States born 1934
Locus 1. 1972
etching and aquatint on folded paper
102.5 x 77.0cm
signed, dated, numbered 35/42
published by Parasol Press, New York
purchased 1981
accession no. 1981. 1006.01

Robert Jacks
Australia born 1943
Paper. 1969
cut paper
182.0 x 122.0cm
unsigned, undated
purchased 1979

Jay McCafferty
United States born 1948, California
To hear it. 1980
burnt paper coloured with inks and synthetic polymer
91.2 x 91.4cm
verso signed, dated, titled
purchased 1982

Caroline Greenwald
United States
Amber wings in frozen clouds. 1982
from *Map* series
laminated tenjugo, gampi, silk and abaca pulp in an amaté portfolio
101.0 x 140.0cm open, 35.0 x 15.0cm folded in portfolio
published by Getler/Pall Gallery, New York
purchased 1982

Alan Shields
United States born 1944, Kansas
TV rerun, A B and C. 1978
embossed linecuts on coloured hand-made paper with applied silver leaf and perforations
each 26.4cm diameter
signed, inscribed 'RTP A', 'RTP B', 'RTP C' (editions each 10)
published by Tyler Graphics Ltd, Bedford Village, New York
purchased 1979
accession nos 1979.2879. 01-03

Roosevelt set from *Box Sweet Jane's egg triumvirate*. 1978
multiple construction made from screenprinted, lithographed and hand-stamped laminated papers in perspex box
box 45.0 x 48.8 x 57.0cm
signed, inscribed 'II RTP' (edition 18)
published by Tyler Graphics Ltd, Bedford Village, New York
purchased 1979
accession no. 1979.2881

Color radar smile B. 1979
etching and aquatint on multicoloured perforated laminated hand-made paper with relief printing on verso
64.4cm square
signed, dated, titled, inscribed RTP
published by Tyler Graphics Ltd, Bedford Village, New York
purchased 1980
accession no. 1980.2039. 02

Dorothea Rockburne
Locus 1. as folded for printing

Dorothea Rockburne
Locus 1. 1972
etching and aquatint on folded paper
102.5 x 77.0cm

Robert Jacks
Paper. 1969
cut paper 182.0 x 122.0cm

Caroline Greenwald
Amber wings in frozen clouds. 1982
from *Map* series
laminated tenjugo, gampi, silk and abaca pulp
in an amaté portfolio
101.0 x 140.0cm open, 35.0 x 15.0cm folded

Alan Shields
TV rerun A. 1978
embossed linecut on coloured hand-made paper with applied silver leaf and perforations
26.4cm diameter

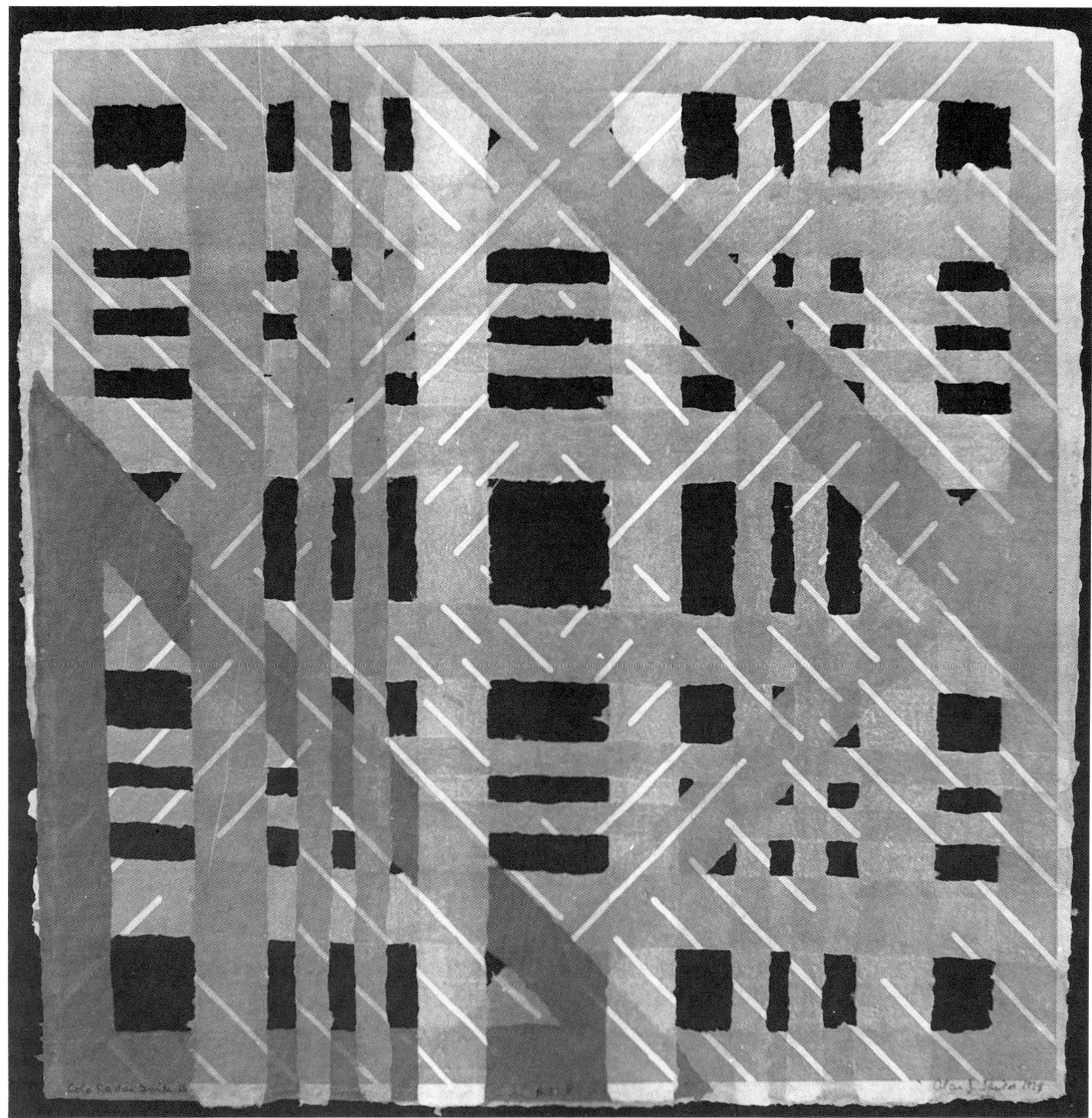

Alan Shields
Color radar smile B. 1979
double-sided intaglio and relief
print on laminated paper
64.4cm square

"It is difficult to ascertain when paper was first used as an independent medium" wrote Jules Heller in his book *Papermaking*. "Most likely it happened in one of those moments when a papermaker decided to pin up his newly made sheet simply because it looked so beautiful".[5]

If one asks where the craftsmanship of paper as a support ceases and the art of presenting the piece of paper one has made as a self-sufficient work begins, it certainly goes back at least as far as Douglass Howell. Already in the 1940s, Howell was painting with coloured pulp; later he exhibited drawings made by embedding pieces of thread in paper at the wet stage.

But in addition to those Americans who took the craft of papermaking and turned it into an art, there were European artists active in manipulating pulp considerably before most Americans. Isabel Echarri of France, for example, was a part of the 'white on white' movement noted in connection with inkless embossing. As early as 1962, she was moulding sculptures and reliefs in colourless paper pulp.

Paper is made either by pulping such fibres as cotton, hemp, or the inner bark of Japanese gampi, kozo or mitsumata shrubs, or by recycling waste paper or rags. The ingredients are cooked and then macerated in a beater until they form a dilute slurry of individual filaments suspended in water. A sieve-like screen, the mould, with a mesh of either woven or parallel laid wires bound together, is dipped into the vat. A layer of the 'stuff' is drawn out and the water drains away, allowing a sheet of matted fibres to settle upon the wire surface. A snug-fitting frame called a deckle, which prevents the fluid pulp running out of the mould and creates the irregular feathering typical of the edge of hand-made paper, is then removed. The paper is tipped or 'couched' onto damp felts and when a 'post' has piled up, the sheets are pressed to extract the water. Mechanization of this process, employing a cylindrical vat and a continuous ribbon of felt, produces a roll rather than individual sheets. The quality of paper however, and its longevity for art purposes, resides not so much in whether it is hand or mould-made, but in the purity of fibre and water and the way they are beaten; for the same basic raw materials can produce both lint-like blotting and translucent glassine.

Once the artist is involved in papermaking, there are limitless possibilities. Coloured sheets can be laminated together, moulds can be shaped to permit the depiction of images in coloured pulps, and the wet or semi-wet paper may be embellished with additives. It can be drawn into with water or liquid dye, deliberately wrinkled and torn, or even sculpturally cast. Such works can be made as one-of-a-kind, or in editions.

Painting with pulp

Although many artists had made paper before him, **Rauschenberg** was perhaps the best-known artist to work with pulp in the early 1970s. The event arranged by Ken Tyler, in which Rauschenberg took over the fourteenth century French Richard de Bas paper mill in Ambert, acted as a catalyst in the United States and was followed by an astonishing upsurge of papermaking activity.

A collaborator who believes that two people with good ideas working together produce more than the same two people working apart, Rauschenberg has tried to maintain the freshness of his approach by continually exploring the unfamiliar. He went to France with two basic ideas — to "allow the form to become the print", and to "paint in paper". During four days of August in 1973, he produced prototypes for five *Pages* and seven *Fuses*, as well as doing part of the editioning. *Page 1*, which incorporated a scrap of cotton rag used to make the pulp, was a completely free form poured onto the mesh without the use of a confining mould. For the other four *Pages*, bleached and unbleached pulps, "looking like bad yoghurt", were mixed in five tonal gradations and formed in moulds a tinsmith had made to the artist's designs. At the end of the project the mill's artisans trampled them with their clogs to effect cancellation![6]

While the *Pages* were relatively colourless, the *Fuses* contained intense Swiss dyes. In addition to spooning coloured pulp into the moulds, Rauschenberg had provided himself with several ready-printed images on coloured tissue — for instance a telegraph pole and a bird in *Link*. These were bonded to the pulp at the wet stage, a feat which Rauschenberg likened to "trying to flatten something on a bubble bath".[7] The title of the series derives from the colour bleeding from one pulp into another when the papers were pressed between felts in the mill's fourteenth century wooden screw press.

Continuing such practices when he moved to his workshop on America's East Coast, Tyler initially collaborated with John Koller who by this time had set up HMP in Connecticut. Koller's studio was used for most of Tyler's earlier paper projects. In 1976, **Ellsworth Kelly** worked for eight months with Tyler and Koller making a series of elegant images by laminating layers of coloured pulp onto white base sheets. Kelly, who refines the shape of a window or the curve of a hill to the point where its deceptively simple abstracted form becomes the content of the work, employed both strong pure primary colours and subtle neutrals, controlling the way these fused and bled when the sheets were pressed.

When **David Hockney**, whom Tyler had long tried to lure to his workshop, saw these "stunningly beautiful" Kelly images in 1978, the visit the painter had intended as a brief pause on his way to California, stretched from August to October as he mastered the new and fascinating medium to which Tyler initiated him.[8]

After some preparatory single sheets featuring sunflowers, Hockney decided to concentrate on water, the representation of which has continually fascinated him.

The *Paper pools* were the result, the most characteristic image a six-sheet frontal view of Tyler's pool from the perspectivally foreshortened diving board. Later the series expanded into a twelve-sheet oblique view of a figure diving into the water. Because the scale was so large, Hockney's sheets had to be couched onto a platform in Tyler's garden.

Technically the works were realized by constructing a framework with 3.75cm (1 1/2 inch) galvanized metal walls based on drawings of Tyler's swimming pool that the artist had enlarged from his own Polaroid photographs. In a process somewhat resembling that used to make cloisonné enamel, Hockney spooned coloured pulp into areas contained by the metal placed over a white base sheet, subsequently adding more colour freehand with tools varying from kitchen baster to airbrush. At times even a hose was called into service and Hockney enjoyed the appropriateness of a watery medium for a watery subject.

Although each *Paper pool* is, strictly speaking, unique, several are inconographically related through the repeated use of comparatively few iron moulds. This puts them in a class similar to the monotypes Whistler and Gauguin would produce by varying the inking of single printing matrices.

As summer changed into autumn, the lido blues and greens mottled and clouded under rain in washy gradations and the same scene became enchanted in four mysterious night variations. It was then that Hockney tackled the paradox of frozen movement and the representation of light in and under the water. The Australian National Gallery's *Diver*, made in three versions, tackles both problems at once.

Hockney was thrilled to work with someone of Tyler's energy and dedication. "With Ken Tyler", he wrote in a book about the project, "nothing was impossible. If I said could we, he said yes, it can be done".[9]

Kenneth Noland had been working with Tyler for five months before Hockney's arrival. In fact it was to allow him scale larger than Koller could accommodate that Tyler now set up his own papermaking studio. Noland is a painter who uses reductive geometric imagery for the exploration of form and colour, stripped of descriptive or literary qualities. In 1953 he had seen Helen Frankenthaler staining thinned acrylic into unsized canvas. By uniting colour and ground, this process emphasized painting's two-dimensional nature as advocated by the formalist art criticism of the period and Nolan adopted the method. Twenty years later, manipulating colour as part of the 'stuff' of paper-making clearly related to staining paint into the fabric of the canvas. Noland, who had never liked printmaking or the idea of multiplying images, fell in love with making paper.

In five months with Tyler, Noland made over 200 images, subtly uniting Western and Oriental fibres and expanding his palette to over a hundred colours by intermixing pulps. As with Hockney, although each work is a unique variant, series were determined by the repeated use of basic moulds. Some of the delicate, atmospheric *Circles* began with beige or peach base sheets onto which Noland smeared, poured and patted additional colours. On top of a ragged circle from a wove mould, transparent rectangular sheets of Oriental fibres 'couched' from a flexible bamboo mould were superimposed, muting the effect. During the making process, bright bits of shredded paper, wool or silk were sprinkled into the wet 'stuff' to emphasize its surface. After drying, monotype lithographic printings were added. The much larger *Diagonal stripe* and *Horizontal stripe* series were made from between two and six layers of more deeply-coloured pulps, enriched by additional staining.

Noland was already a seasoned papermaker when he worked with Tyler, having taken up the process two years earlier in 1976 when Garner Tullis, of the International Institute of Experimental Printmaking had invited him to participate as master-in-residence at a paper workshop. Noland became so enthusiastic that he set up his own studio.

Tullis came to paper quite independent of the development elsewhere in America and himself casts paper sculpture. He has collaborated with many artists at his elaborately-equipped workshop in California. One of them was **Joe Zucker**, whose paintings have been described as having "the light heartedness and vulgarity of an amusement park".[10] Zucker's unusual painting method, of adhering cotton balls dipped in acrylic colour to a cotton support, translated very directly into paperwork. Screenprinting an edition of his favourite image of a toucan as a guide onto paper, Zucker worked over it with dyed cotton pulp mixed with organic glue, making twenty-five unique but related works.

Tullis also taught six Gemini technicians to make paper before they worked with **Keith Sonnier** in 1976. Sonnier, who has worked in neon, video, sound and film, introduced into his sculptural vocabulary in 1968 large fabricated square and circular pieces of glass. There shapes recur in his *Abaca code* — paperworks made in each of three gigantic formats. Abaca is the name of a plant cultivated in the Philippines and used by Sonnier as one of his ingredients. Black and red cotton rags (the latter from discarded restaurant napkins) were combined with natural-coloured fibres to make the paper 'stuff' poured into the outsize moulds. After drying, the paper shapes — which were one inch thick in places — were printed with metal stamps pounded in by sledge hammer, so that the number of each piece, the date in Roman numerals, and the artist's initials became an integral part of the image.

William Weege, has made paperworks with the assistance of Tullis in California and of Joe Wilfer at the Upper U.S. Paper Mill in Wisconsin. As an artist, Weege has always attacked the conventions. In the 1960s his weapons were photo-offset protest prints rushed out in response to political events. More recently he has concentrated on attacking aesthetic conventions, making a funky unique series of paper pieces by raising coloured pulp from the vat in shreds, using cat's cradles of string in place of a mould, and pressing offbeat forms together.

After several years running his own mill, Wilfer transferred to New York and the Dieu Donne press where last year he worked with the photo-realist, **Chuck Close**.

Close, who is fascinated by the ability of photography to nail down blur, makes large-scale paintings of friends painstakingly built up on an underlying but usually invisible cellular grid. In his prints, Close has often allowed that structural grid to show. Three paperworks featuring Keith, a friend who has often appeared in Close's graphic work, were built up in 1.5cm squares of pulp in various shades of grey, inlaid on white, grey or black base sheets. As the viewer steps back, this abstract tesselation of 1,496 squares magically becomes Keith.

Sculpting pulp

In addition to being a pioneer in the two-dimensional aspects of paper, Howell was in the vanguard of sculpted paper as well. In 1952 he introduced the medium to Harold Paris, who now makes very large scale three-dimensional pieces, while in the mid-1960s he helped Michael Ponce de León, influenced in his collage intaglio work by Rolf Nesch, to construct a spiralling paper mould for a three-dimensional print that was quite exceptional in its day.

It was **Robert Rauschenberg** once again who established the trend. He followed his experiences in a French mill by going to Ahmedabad in India, where a wealthy family had invited him to work on any project of his choosing. A large textile centre, Ahmedabad was the birth-place of Gandhi who, on behalf of local workers, had organized several ashrams where members of the poorest caste could learn craft skills. The papermaking facility in which Rauschenberg chose to work was one of these, and *Bones and unions* were made there. The *Bones* were made by sandwiching cuttings of local cloth and bamboo slats as inlays between two layers of rag paper formed in moulds he designed. The *Unions* were of a substance Rauschenberg invented with local help which he called 'rag mud'. This he blended from paper pulp and the adobe mud used for traditional house building. The mud includes various aromatic ingredients as insect repellants, so the multiples appeal to the smell among other aesthetic senses. In true collaborative spirit, the names of Ram, Khilji, Das and other Indian workers who assisted in the project appear alongside that of Rauschenberg in the Gemini documentation.

Frank Stella also undertook a three-dimensional paper project during 1975, working with Tyler and Koller in Connecticut for fifteen months. His flat ascetic compositions had by then changed for more exuberant geometries which gradually moved out into three dimensions. His paper reliefs stemmed from a series of 1970 drawings with titles commemorating eighteenth century wooden synagogues, remarkably Constructivist in appearance, which were destroyed in Poland and Russia during the Second World War. Various works were made based on these drawings, progressing from flatness through low relief to tilted interlocking planes. For his paper-works, shaped hand-sewn brass screens were dipped into the vat to form papers with sculptural dimension. While still wet, the artist applied dyes and hand-made paper collage. After drying, Stella painted each work, creating 130 variations based on the five basic formats.

Stella has influenced **Lynda Benglis**, the essentials of whose work have been described as an interest in frozen gesture, an eccentric and expressionist use of process and pleasure in vulgarity. Allowing matter to find its own form, she has often worked with fluid materials which later harden. Cast paper has extended such preoccupations. The *Aquanots* were made with the help of Steve Kasher at Bummy Huss paper in New York from fourteen moulds of plastic foam, cast, often more than once, in pigmented cotton pulp. Twenty-five variant combinations resulted, each coloured differently, some with gold leaf and glitter.

Louise Nevelson's fame as a sculptress stems from wall assemblages of wooden elements in boxed compartments, often made from junk or discarded furniture and unified by coats of black, white, or gold paint. Since the mid-1970s, Garner Tullis has produced editions of cast paper reliefs for her. The artist sends a wooden plate by mail, Tullis makes a latex negative and submits proofs. Once approved, the shape is editioned in dye cotton pulp — dark blue in the case of *Night star.*

Cast paper (from which the Victorians even made furniture) has been used not only for abstract images, but for representation. **Claes Oldenburg**, famous for his monuments of vastly inflated nails, lipsticks, legs or ice cream cones, editioned an outsize button in this way.

Works of recycled pulp

Recycling used materials is a traditional method of making paper and many artists have acknowledged this in their work. Some have taken it to extremes. **Joel Fisher** once starved himself for five days, then masticated paper, including a banknote, and formed art from the result. On another occasion, having acquired a macabre new set of clothes vacated by an acquaintance who had hanged himself, Fisher pulped his own wardrobe and exhibited his recycled clothing as a paper environment. Fascinated by 'blankness' and by process becoming the image, Fisher's *First etching* was made from the pulped prints of two other artists representing opposite ends of the aesthetic spectrum.

Silvie Turner, who by chance acquired an edition of another artist's rejected screenprints on their way to the dustbin, tore them up systematically, pulping the lightest parts together and the darkest parts together, with a series of gradations in between. The resulting sheets are juxtaposed as a series of tonal values. Her little pamphlet, *The colours of the times*, is made from recycling those London newspapers or periodicals with 'Times' in their titles. These mostly contribute subtle porridge shades, but for the pale pink of the *Financial Times*, the misleading colour symbolism of which contradicts its high Tory content.

Newsprint was also recycled by **Bea Maddock** for a series of works she made in which she wanted to retain words sitting on the sheet. Working in a quite primitive way, she beat her pulp in a domestic washing machine and used fly screens from her windows as moulds, pressing her irregularly formed sheets between canvas in a bookbinder's press. The title alludes to the fact that too much of the background intruded when the newspaper image of Ann Frank was photocopied by the artist.

Watermark as image

Watermarks have for centuries been made in paper by stitching initials or an image drawn in wire over the mesh of the mould so that the slurry of pulp settling on it from the vat will be thinner at that point. This enables the identity of the paper to be read against the light and often reveals to the historian where and when a paper was made.

Clinton Hill has been making paper in collaboration with John Koller since 1974. Hill's works often encompass sequences of separate sheets connected by lines moving from one to another. The artist stitches wires and pieces of plastic into his moulds to produce holes, translucent layers and lacy areas within the sheets, as well as spooning coloured pulps into areas defined by paper templates over newly-formed wet sheets. As in so many paperworks, the history of the way the image was made is apparent.

Ian Tyson started the Tetrad Press in London in 1970 as an imprint under which he could publish significant contemporary poetry, often accompanied by his austere and beautiful abstract images based on subtle adjustments of a grid. Tyson's minimal images are often difficult to show, because they rely on subtle qualities of paper and surface — one white printed on a slightly different white, for example, an effect which may be lost behind glass.

Sign is no exception. The image exists only as a thinner layer of paper within a hand-made sheet, created by selectively building up the surface of the wire mould with which it was made.

Postscript simulated hand-made paper

At the height of the American 'paper revolution', it was often asked whether papermaking was merely a fad, or offered infinite possibilities which artists would continue to develop. Certainly by the late 1970s, there seemed to be scarcely an art school in the Western world without a bath of paper pulp in the corner or an artist whose hands were not in a vat.

In 1979, **Patrick Caulfield**, whose sense of fun has often allowed him a witty dig at artistic trends, took a long slow look at the rising tide of paper pulp, especially its folksier aspects in which corn husks and feathers were embedded in wet sheets. He decided that while it might not be for him it ought not to go unremarked. Enjoying the conceit of mass producing identicality in a fictive 'hand-made' product, he proceeded to place a series of characteristically impassive still lives on backgrounds imitating Japanese paper, kindly screen-printed by Kelpra Studio, London.

Painting with pulp

Robert Rauschenberg
United States born 1925, Texas
Page 1 and Page 3 from *Pages and fuses*. 1974
hand-made paper, Page 1 incorporating cotton rag
38.0 x 51.4cm and 46.4 x 48.4cm irreg.
right to print impressions (editions 27 and 35) both with embossed signature and 'RTP' 74' on verso
published by Gemini G.E.L., Los Angeles
purchased 1975

Link, Hind and Bit from *Pages and fuses*. 1974
hand-made paper of dyed pulp with laminated screenprinted tissue
61.4 x 52.7; 66.0 x 51.0; 47.0 x 48.2cm respectively
right to print impressions signed and dated on verso (editions 29, 34, 33 respectively)
published by Gemini G.E.L., Los Angeles
purchased 1975

Ellsworth Kelly
United States born 1923, New York State
Colored paper images. 1976
coloured pulp fused to base sheet
I-XII measuring 117.0 x 82.0cm;
XIII-XX measuring 81.0 x 78.0cm
each signed, undated, inscribed 'RTP' (editions from 17 to 24)
published by Tyler Graphics Ltd, Bedford Village, New York
purchased 1977

Blue/green/yellow/orange/red. 1977
coloured pulp fused to base sheet
34.0 x 116.6cm
purchased 1977
accession no. 1979.2937

David Hockney
Great Britain born 1937, Bradford
Paper pools. 1978
Steps with shadow, 2-H. 130.0 x 86.8cm
Green pool with diving board and shadow, 3-I. 128.8 x 82.1cm
Gregory in the pool, 4-G. 85.4 x 129.0cm
A diver, 17. 12 sheets each 91.6 x 74.0cm
coloured paper pulp fused to base sheet
all signed, dated, numbered
published by Tyler Graphics Ltd, Bedford Village, New York
purchased 1979
accession nos 1979.2887; 1979.2886; 1979.2888; 1979.2343.01-12

Kenneth Noland
United States born 1924, North Carolina
Circles I-2, I-44, I-52 and II-55 from *Handmade papers* series. 1978
layered coloured western and oriental pulp with monotype lithographic printings
each 51.0 x 41.0cm (vertical and horizontal formats)
each signed, dated, numbered
published by Tyler Graphics Ltd, Bedford Village, New York
purchased 1979
accession nos 1979.2898; 1979.2894; 1979.2899; 1979.2896
Horizontal stripes II-12 and III-19 from *Handmade papers* series. 1978
layered coloured paper pulp with monotype printing and staining
128.2 x 87.4 and 127.4 x 84.2cm respectively
signed, dated, numbered
published by Tyler Graphics Ltd, Bedford Village, New York
purchased 1979
accession nos 1979.2902; 1979.2900

Joe Zucker
United States born 1941, Chicago
Toucan no.17 and Toucan no.19. 1980
from a series of 25 paperworks
dyed cotton pulp applied over screenprint
each 83.0cm square
each signed, dated
published by Pace Editions Inc., New York
purchased 1981
accession nos 1981.2199; 1981.2200

Keith Sonnier
United States born 1941, Louisiana
C-IX, R-IX, and S-IX from *Abaca code* series. 1976
relief printed cast-paper pulp in each of 3 formats
circle: 198.0cm diameter; rectangle: 181.0 x 241.0cm; square: 198.0cm
inscription as image (editions each 10)
published by Gemini G.E.L., Los Angeles
purchased 1978
accession nos 1979.2492; 1979.2493; 1979.2491

William Weege
United States born 1935, Wisconsin
XPTOMP. 1981
pressed dyed paper construction from a series of 100 unique works
60.0 x 80.0cm
published by Pace Editions Inc., New York
purchased 1982

Chuck Close
United States born 1940, Washington
Edition F (black Keith). 1981
laminated pulp (edition 20)
86.0 x 66.0cm
published by Pace Editions Inc., New York
purchased 1982

Sculpting pulp

Robert Rauschenberg
United States born 1925, Texas
Snake eyes, Pit boss and Hard eight from *Bones and unions*. 1975
multiples of cotton rag pulp, cotton fabric and bamboo slats
85.0 x 67.0 x 10.5cm; 86.5 x 69.0 x 8.0cm; 65.8 x 85.0 x 7.0cm respectively
signed, dated, numbered AP VI/XI (editions 33, 28, 32 respectively)
published by Gemini G.E.L., Los Angeles
purchased 1977

Capitol and Charter from *Bones and unions*. 1975
Multiples of paper pulp and adobe mud with bamboo, silk, etc.
80.0 x 112.5 x 10.0cm and 211.0 x 78.0 x 8.0cm
signed, numbered AP7 and AP7 on verso (editions 10 and 15)
published by Gemini G.E.L., Los Angeles
purchased 1977

Frank Stella
United States born 1936, Massachusetts
Kozangrodek (II) and Grodno (I) from *Paper reliefs*. 1975
cast paper with collage and hand colouring
65.2 x 56.4cm and 64.2 x 53.6cm respectively irreg.
signed, dated (editions 26 each of 5 formats)
published by Tyler Graphics Ltd, Bedford Village, New York

Lynda Benglis
United States born 1941, Louisiana
Aquanot no.22. 1981
one of 25 cast-paper reliefs coloured with ink and polymer
159.2 x 80.0 x 16.0cm
signed and dated on verso
co-published by Brooke Alexander Inc. and Paula Cooper Gallery, New York
purchased 1981
accession no. 1981.2206

Louise Nevelson
Russia/United States born 1899
Night star. 1981
dyed cast paper (edition 90)
88.0 x 100.0cm
published by Pace Editions Inc., New York
purchased 1982

Claes Oldenburg
Sweden/United States born 1925, Stockholm
Button. 1981
cast paper, screenprinted board
(edition 100)
41.5 x 36.0 x 16.5cm
published by Multiples Inc., New York
purchased 1982

Works of recycled pulp

Joel Fisher
United States born 1947, Ohio
First etching. 1980
blind debossing on recycled paper
68.5 x 137.0cm
(edition 25)
published by Crown Point Press, Oakland, California
purchased 1982

Silvie Turner
Great Britain born 1946, Yorkshire
Grey scale. 1981
hand-made recycled paper
6 overlapping sheets each 40.0 x 30.0cm
signed, numbered 10/10
purchased 1982

Colours of the times. 1981
recycled pulp from newspapers and periodicals
small bookwork, open 32.0 x 46.5cm
artist's proof (edition 50)
purchased 1982

Bea Maddock
Australia born 1934
Too much comes from the back. 1975
half-tone relief etching on pulped newsprint
trial proof 24.8 x 30.8cm
loaned by the artist

Watermark as image

Clinton Hill
United States born 1922, Idaho
Black track. 1978
hand-made paper with watermarks and dyed pulp
57.0 x 185.0cm
published by Marilyn Pearl Gallery, New York
purchased 1982

Ian Tyson
Great Britain born 1933, Yorkshire
Sign. 1981
rag pulp with watermark as image
33.0 x 30.5cm
couched by Susan Hostetler at
Jin Paper, Friedberg (edition 90)
published by Edition Hoffmann, West Germany
purchased 1982

Postscript — simulated hand-made paper

Patrick Caulfield
Great Britain born 1936, London
Cream glazed pot, Fruit and bowl, Plant pot. 1979/80
screenprints on imitated oriental paper
each 84.0 x 59.6cm
signed, undated, each inscribed 7/100
published by Waddington Graphics, London
purchased 1980
accession nos 1980.780-782

Robert Rauschenberg
Link. 1974
from *Pages and fuses* series
hand-made paper of dyed pulp with laminated
screenprinted tissue
61.4 x 52.7cm

Ellsworth Kelly
Colored paper image X. 1976
coloured pulp fused to base sheet
117.0 x 82.0cm

David Hockney
Green pool with diving board
and shadow, 3-I. 1978
from *Paper pools* series
coloured paper pulp fused to base sheet
128.8 x 82.1cm

David Hockney
A diver, 17. 1978
from *Paper pools* series
coloured paper pulp fused to base sheet
12 sheets each 91.6 x 74.0cm

David Hockney
Steps with shadow 2-H. 1978
from *Paper pools* series
coloured paper pulp fused to base sheet
130.0 x 86.8cm

Kenneth Noland
Circle 1-2. 1978
from *Handmade paper* series
layered coloured western and oriental pulp with
monotype lithographic printings
51.0 x 41.0cm

Kenneth Noland
Horizontal stripes II-12. 1978
from *Handmade papers* series
layered coloured paper pulps with
monotype printing and staining
128.2 x 87.4cm

Joe Zucker
Toucan no.19. 1980
from a series of 25 paperworks
dyed cotton pulp applied over screenprint
83.0cm square

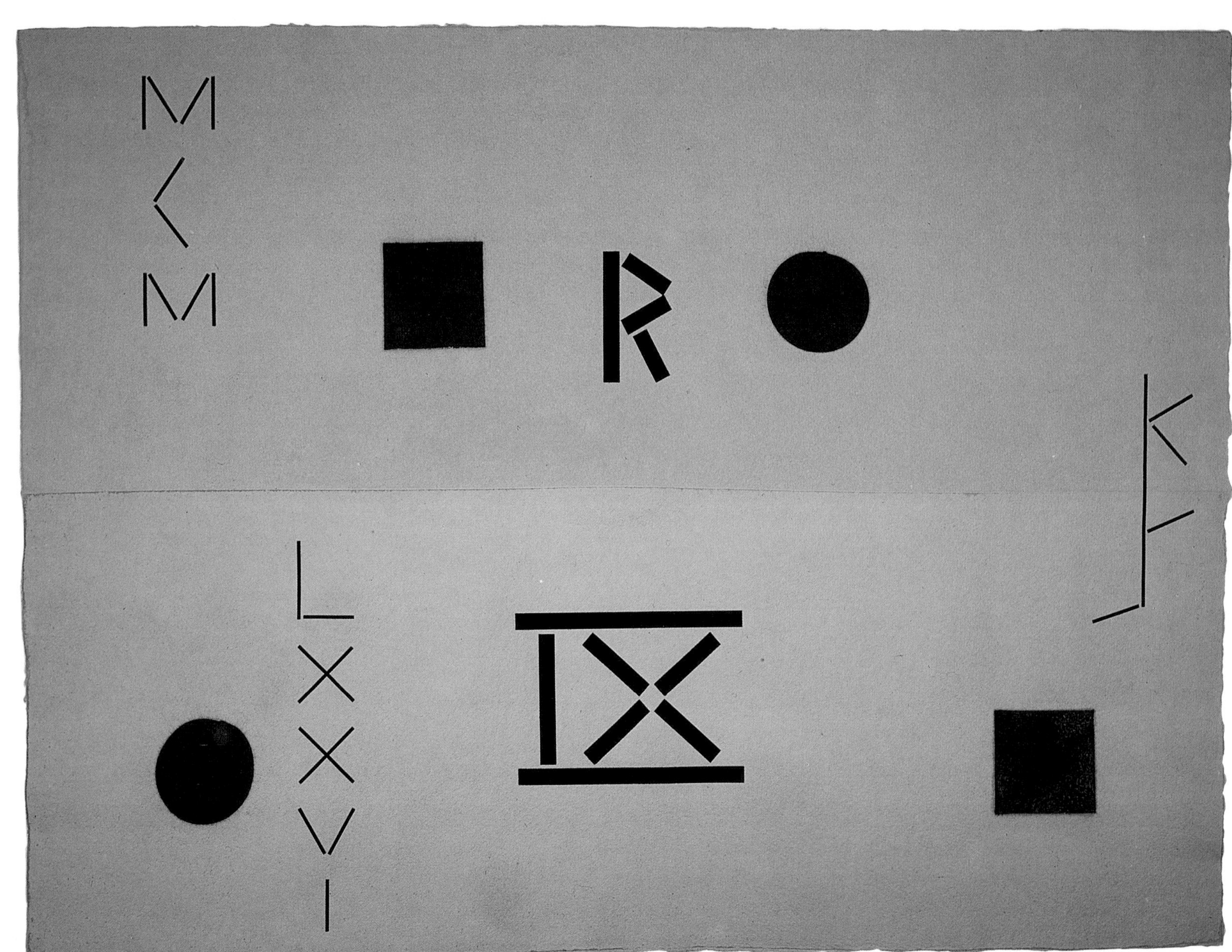

Keith Sonnier
R-IX. 1976
from *Abaca code* series
relief printed cast-paper pulp
181.0 x 241.0cm

Chuck Close
Edition F (black Keith). 1981
laminated pulp
86.0 x 66.0cm

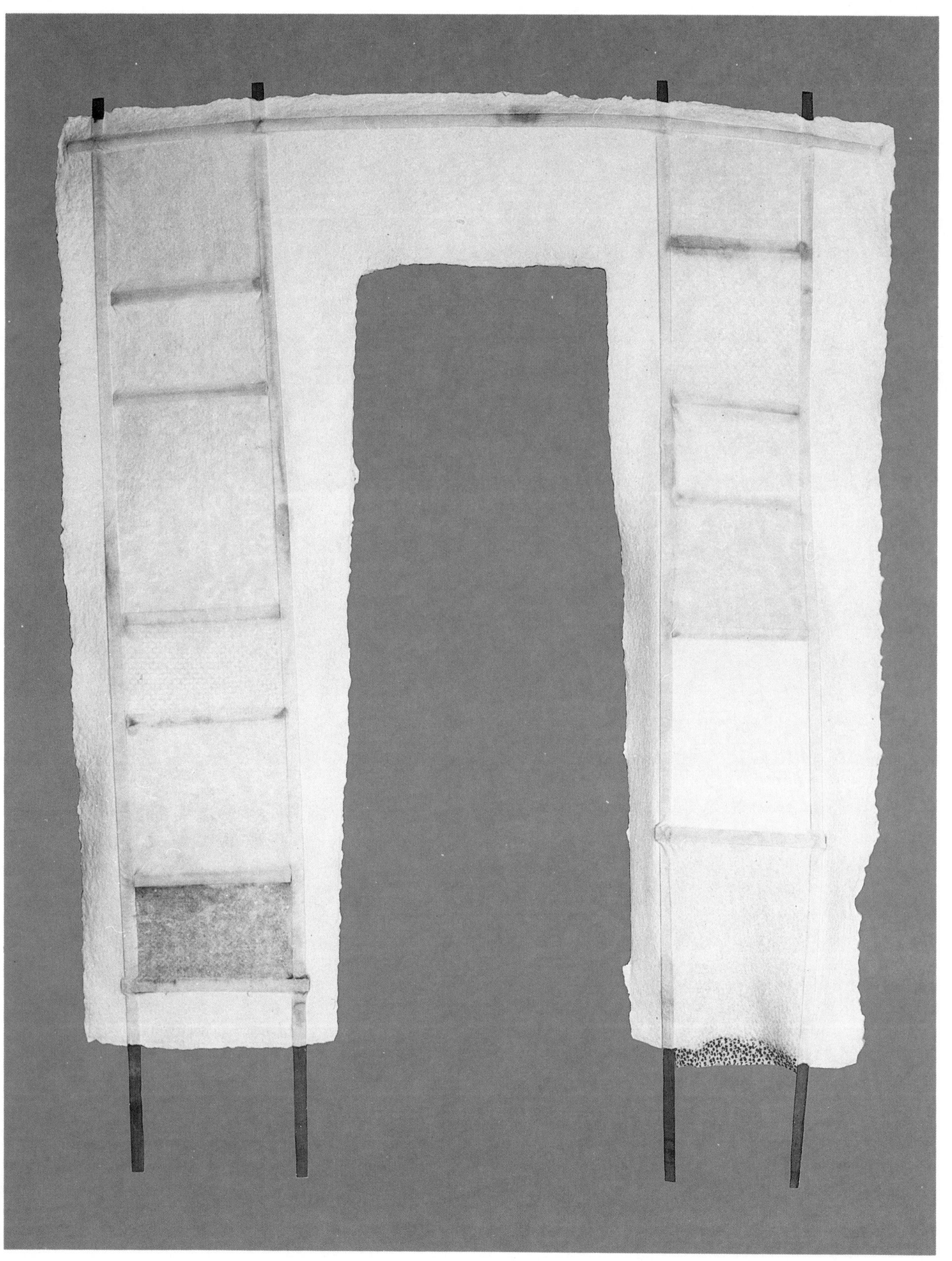

Robert Rauschenberg
Snake eyes. 1975
from *Bones and unions*
multiple of cotton rag pulp,
cotton fabric and
bamboo slats
85.0 x 67.0 x 10.5cm

Robert Rauschenberg
Capitol. 1975
from *Bones and unions*
multiple of paper pulp and adobe mud with
bamboo, wood, silk, glass
80.0 x 112.5 x 10.0cm

Frank Stella
Grodno I. 1975
from *Paper reliefs*
cast paper with collage and hand colouring
64.2 x 53.6cm

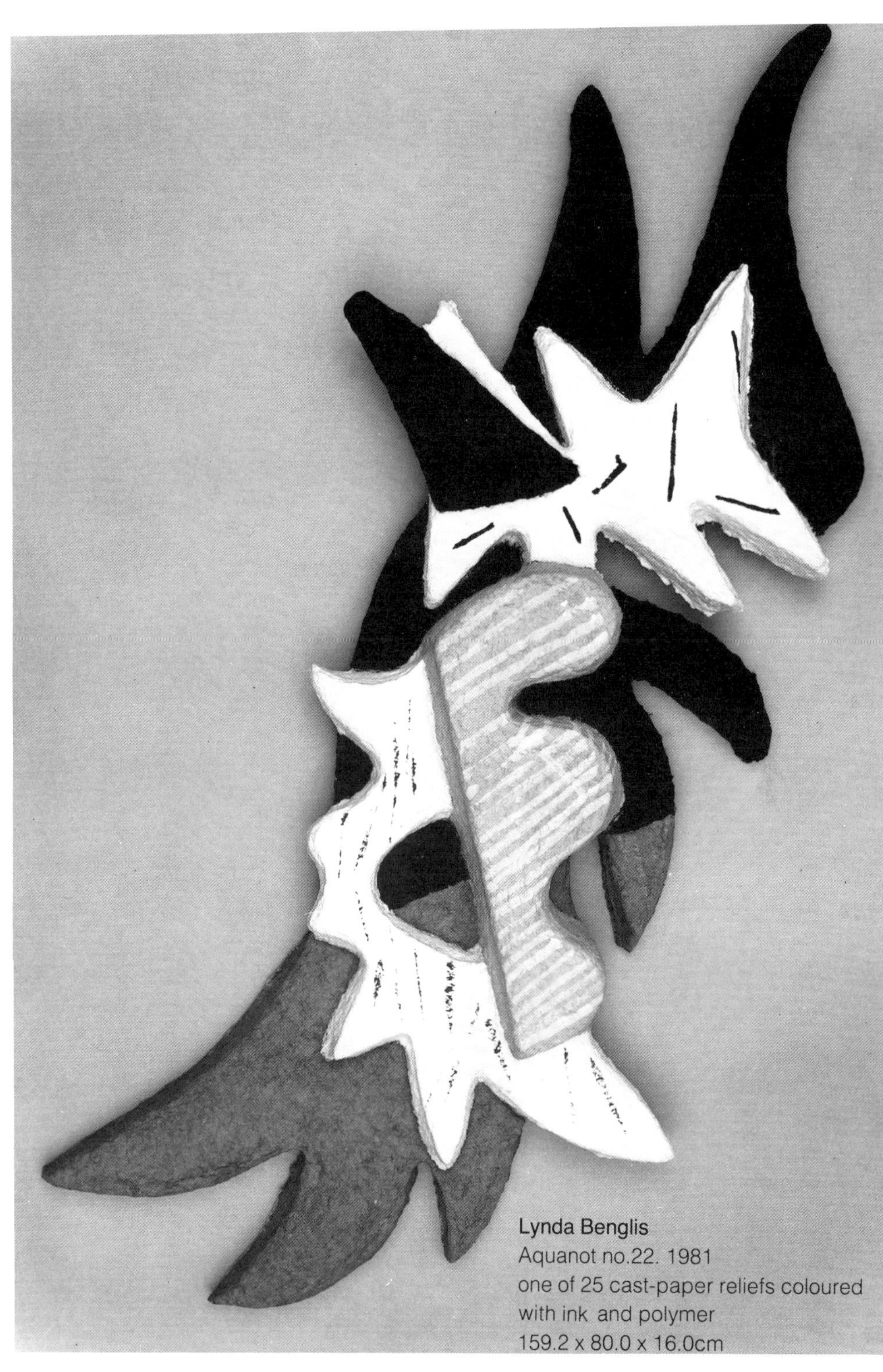

Lynda Benglis
Aquanot no.22. 1981
one of 25 cast-paper reliefs coloured with ink and polymer
159.2 x 80.0 x 16.0cm

Silvie Turner
Grey scale. 1981
hand-made recycled paper
6 overlapping sheets
each 40.0 x 30.0cm

Silvie Turner
Colours of the times. 1981
recycled pulp from newspapers and periodicals
small bookwork 32.0 x 46.5cm open

Bea Maddock
Too much comes from the back. 1975
half-tone relief etching on pulped newsprint
trial proof 24.8 x 30.8cm

Clinton Hill
Black track. 1978
hand-made paper with watermarks and dyed pulp
57.0 x 185.0cm

Ian Tyson
Sign. 1981
rag pulp with watermark as image
33.0 x 30.5cm

Patrick Caulfield
Cream glazed pot. 1979-80
screenprint on imitated Japanese paper
84.0 x 59.6cm

Patrick Caulfield
Fruit and bowl. 1979-80
screenprint on imitated Japanese paper
84.0 x 59.6cm

Bibliography

Books, catalogues, articles on papermaking by artists

Albright Knox Art Gallery, New York. *With Paper, About Paper*. New York, The Gallery, 1980. Introduction by Charlotta Kotik. (Exhibition catalogue).

American Artist. Vol.41, No.421. Aug. 1977, pp.33-49.

Heller, Jules. *Papermaking*. New York, Watson-Guptill, 1978.**(5)**

Kasher, Steven. 'The Substance of Paper'. *Artforum*. March 1978, pp.27-28.**(4)**

Leopold Hoesch Museum, Düren. *Das Papier*. Düren, The Museum, May-July 1981. (Exhibition catalogue).

Print Collector's Newsletter. Vol.10, No.3. July-Aug. 1979. pp.73-86.

Rotterdam. 'de Doelen'. *Papier, Als Beeldend Middel*. Rotterdam, de Doelen, 1980-81. (Exhibition catalogue).

Santa Barbara Museum of Art. *The Handmade Paper Object*. Santa Barbara, The Museum, Oct.-Nov. 1976. Introduction by Richard Kubiak. (Exhibition catalogue).

Smithsonian Institution, Washington, D.C. *New Ways with Paper*. Washington D.C., National Collection of Fine Arts, Dec. 1977-Feb. 1978. Introduction by Jane Flint. (Exhibition catalogue).

Smithsonian Institution, Washington, D.C. *Paper as Medium*. Washington D.C., Smithsonian Institution Travelling Exhibition Service, 1980. Introduction by Jane M. Farmer. (Exhibition catalogue).

Washington, D.C. National Gallery of Art. *Paper in Prints*. Washington, D.C., The Gallery, 1977. Introduction by Andrew Robison. (Exhibition catalogue).

World Print Council. *Paper — Art and Technology*. San Francisco, 1979.

Albers, A.

Bayer, H. (et al). *Bauhaus 1919-1928*. New York, Museum of Modern Art, 1938. (Paperback reprint : London, Secker and Warburg, 1975).
Brooklyn Museum. *Anni Albers*. Brooklyn, The Museum, 1977. Introduction by N. Fox Weber. (Exhibition catalogue).

Albers, J.

Albers, J. *Interaction of Colour*. New Haven and London, Yale University Press, 1963.
Bayer, H. (et al). *Bauhaus 1919-1928*. New York, Museum of Modern Art, 1938. (Paperback reprint : London, Secker and Warburg, 1975).
Gemini G.E.L. *Josef Albers : Embossed Linear Constructions*. Los Angeles, Gemini, 1969. Introduction by Sheldon Nodelman. (Catalogue).**(1)**
Washington, D.C. Gallery of Modern Art. *Josef Albers : The American Years*. Washington, D.C., The Gallery, 1965. Introduction by Gerald Norland. (Exhibition catalogue).

Benglis, L.

Pincus-Witten, Robert. 'Lynda Benglis : The Frozen Gesture'. *Artforum*. Nov.1974, pp.54-59.
Print Collector's Newsletter. Vol.9, No.5, Nov.-Dec. 1978, p.164; Vol.10, No.3, July-Aug. 1979, pp.94-95; Vol.12, No.1, March-April 1981, p.22.

Caulfield, P.

Finch, Christopher. *Patrick Caulfield*. Harmondsworth, Penguin, 1971.
Tate Gallery, London. *Patrick Caulfield - Paintings of 1963-1981*. London, The Gallery, 1981. (Exhibition catalogue).
Waddington Graphics. *Patrick Caulfield Prints 1964-1981*. London, Waddington, 1981. Introduction by Bryan Robertson. (Exhibition catalogue).

Close, C.

Arts Council of Great Britain, London. *Photo-Realism*. London, Serpentine Gallery, April-May 1973. (Exhibition catalogue).
Print Collector's Newsletter. Vol.12, No.5, Nov.-Dec. 1981, p.150.
Shapiro, Michael. 'Changing Variables : Chuck Close and His Prints'. *Print Collector's Newsletter*. Vol.9, No.3, July-Aug. 1978, pp.69-73.

Dumont, M.

William Weston Gallery, London. *Maurice Dumont 1870-1899 — Symbolist Aquatints, Relief Prints and Lithographs*. London, The Gallery, Year 14, Issue 153, 1981. (Catalogue).

Fisher, J.

Art and Artists. Jan. 1972, pp.32-37. (Interview transcript : Simon Field with Joel Fisher).

Greenwald, C.

Farmer, Jane M. 'Poems of Land and Sky'. *Print Collector's Newsletter*. Vol.10, No.3, July-Aug. 1979, pp.77-79.

Hagiwara, H.

McCaughey, Patrick. 'Hideo Hagiwara'. *Art and Australia*. Vol.6, No.2, 1968, pp.126-130.
Petit, Gaston. *Forty-Four Japanese Print Artists*. Japan, Kobansha International, 1973.
Robertson, Ronald. *Contemporary Printmaking in Japan*. New York, Crown, 1965.

Hayter, S.W.

Gilmour, Pat. 'Prints U.S.A. 1982'. *Print Review*. New York, 1982, pp.11-18. (Interview transcript : Pat Gilmour with Stanley William Hayter).
Hayter, S.W. *New Ways in Gravure*. New York, Pantheon, 1949.
Hayter, S.W. *About Prints*. London, Oxford University Press, 1962.
Oxford Gallery. *For S.W. Hayter on his 80th Birthday*. Oxford, The Gallery, 1981. Introduction by Pat Gilmour. (Exhibition catalogue).
Victoria and Albert Museum, London. *Engravings of S.W. Hayter*. London, HMSO, 1967. (Exhibition catalogue).
Whitechapel Art Gallery, London. *S.W. Hayter Retrospective 1927-57*. London, The Gallery, 1957. Introduction by Bryan Robertson. (Exhibition catalogue).

Hill, C.

Gilbert-Rolfe, Jeremy. 'Clinton Hill'. *Artforum*. Sept. 1979, pp.68-69.
Montclair Art Museum, New Jersey. *Clinton Hill — Paintings and Paperworks*. New Jersey, The Museum, 1981. Text by Martica Sawin. (Exhibition catalogue).

Hockney, D.

Butterfield, Jan. 'David Hockney : Blue Hedonistic Pools'. *Print Collector's Newsletter*. Vol.10, No.3, July-Aug. 1979, pp.73-76.
Hockney, David. *Paper Pools*. London, Thames and Hudson, 1980.**(8)(9)**
Print Collector's Newsletter. Vol.10, No.1, March-April 1979, pp.19-20.
Stangos, Nikos (ed.). *David Hockney by David Hockney*. London, Thames and Hudson, 1976.

Johns, J.

Bernstein, Roberta. 'Johns and Beckett : Foirades/Fizzles'. *Print Collector's Newsletter*. Vol.7, No.5, Nov.-Dec. 1976, pp.141-145.
Davison Art Gallery, Middletown, Connecticut. *Jasper Johns : Prints 1970-1977*. Middletown, Conn., Wesleyan University, 1978. (Exhibition catalogue).
Field, Richard S. *Jasper Johns : Prints 1960-1970*. Philadelphia Museum of Art, and Praeger, 1970.

Kelly, E.

Amsterdam, Stedlijk Museum. *Ellsworth Kelly — Paintings & Sculptures 1963-1979*. Amsterdam, The Museum, 1979-1980. (Exhibition catalogue).
Gemini G.E.L. *Kelly*. Los Angeles, Gemini, 1970. Introduction by John Coplans. (Catalogue)
Waldman, Diane. *Ellsworth Kelly, Drawings, Collages, Prints*. Greenwich, Connecticut, New York Graphic Society, 1971.

Wortz, Melinda. 'New Editions (Twelve Leaves)'. *Art News*. Sept. 1978, p.106.

Lichtenstein, Roy

Coplans, John. *Roy Lichtenstein*. New York, Praeger, 1972.
Tate Gallery, London. *Roy Lichtenstein*. London, The Gallery, 1968. Introduction by R. Morphet. (Exhibition catalogue).

McCafferty, J.

Dunham, Judith. 'Making Art with the Sun'. *Artweek*. June 1976, p.6.
Knight, Christopher. 'Jay McCafferty, Cirrus Gallery'. *Artforum*. May 1980, p.85.

Moser, K.

Fisher Fine Art Ltd, London. *Vienna Turn of the Century Art and Design*. London, Fisher Fine Art, 1979-80. (Catalogue).

Motherwell, R.

Colsman-Freyberger, Heidi. 'Robert Motherwell — Words & Images'. *Print Collector's Newsletter*. Vol.4, No.6, Jan.-Feb. 1974, pp.124-129.
Sandler, Irving. *The Triumph of American Painting : A History of Abstract Expressionism*. New York, Harper & Row, 1970.
Terenzio, S. *The Painter and the Printer — Robert Motherwell's Graphics 1943-1980*. New York, American Federation of the Arts, 1980. (Catalogue raisonné by D. Belknap).**(3)**

Nevelson, L.

Albright, Thomas. 'The Spirit of Santa Cruz'. *Art News*. Jan. 1976, pp.52-56. *Print Collector's Newsletter*. Vol.7, No.1, March-April 1976, p.24.

Noland, K.

Goldman, Judith. *Kenneth Noland : Hand-made papers*. New York, Tyler Graphics, 1978. (Catalogue).
Moffet, Kenworth. *Kenneth Noland*. New York, Abrams, 1977.

Oldenburg, C.

Goldman, Judith. 'Sort of a Commercial for Objects'. *Print Collector's Newsletter*. Vol.2, No.6, Jan.-Feb. 1972, p.117.
Stockholm. Moderna Museet. *Claes Oldenburg, Drawings, Watercolours, Prints*. Stockholm, The Museum, 1977. (Exhibition catalogue).

Rauschenberg, R.

Alloway, Lawrence. 'Rauschenberg's Graphics'. *Art and Artists*. Sept. 1970, pp. 18-21.
Arts Council of Great Britain. *Pages and Fuses and Other Prints by Robert Rauschenberg*. London, Arts Council of Great Britain, 1975. (Exhibition broadsheet).
Forge, Andrew. *Rauschenberg*. New York, Abrams, 1969.
Gemini G.E.L. *Cardbirds*. Los Angeles, Gemini, 1971. (Catalogue).**(2)**
Gemini G.E.L. *Pages and Fuses*. Los Angeles, Gemini, 1974. (Catalogue).**(6)**
Saff, Donald. 'Graphics Studio USF'. *Art Journal*. Fall, 1974, pp.10-18.
Washington, D.C. National Collection of Fine Arts. *Robert Rauschenberg*. Washington, Smithsonian Institute, 1976. (Exhibition catalogue).
Young, Joseph. 'Pages and Fuses: An Extended View of Robert Rauschenberg'. *Print Collector's Newsletter*. Vol.5, No.2, May-June 1974, pp.25-30.**(7)**

Roche, P.

Battersby, M. *Art Nouveau*. Feltham, Middlesex, Hamlyn, 1969.

Rockburne, D.

Bochner, Mel. 'A note on Dorothea Rockburne'. *Artforum*. March 1972, p.28.
Licht, Jennifer. 'An Interview with Dorothea Rockburne.' *Artforum*. March 1972, pp.34-36.
Olsen, Roberta. 'An Interview with Dorothea Rockburne'. *Art in America*. Nov.-Dec. 1978, pp.141-145.
Ontario. Art Gallery. *Prints : Bochner, Le Witt, Mangold, Marden, Martin, Renouf, Rockburne, Ryman*. Ontario, The Gallery, Dec. 1975-Jan. 1976. (Exhibition catalogue).
Pincus-Witten, Robert. 'Mel and Dorothea : Rehearsing One's Coolness'. *Arts Magazine*. Nov. 1978, pp.121-129.
Ratcliff, Carter, 'Dorothea Rockburne: New Prints'. *Print Collector's Newsletter*. Vol.5, No.2, May-June 1974, pp.30-32.
Rockburne, Dorothea. 'Works and Statements'. *Artforum*. March 1972, pp.29-33.

Shields, A.

Kelder, Diane. 'Things with Printmaking Techniques'. *Art in America*. May 1973, pp.86-88.
Pindell, Howardena. 'Tales of Brave
Ulysses : Alan Shields Interviewed'. *Print Collector's Newsletter*. Vol.5, No.6, Jan.-Feb. 1975, pp.143-157.

Skiold, B.

Gilmour, Pat. 'Birgit Skiold : Zen Gardens'. *Arts Review*. Nov. 1973.
Skiold, Birgit and Turner, S. *Handmade Paper Today*. London, Lund Humphries, due 1982.
Spencer, Charles. *Birgit Skiold*. London, Editions Alecto, 1973. Alecto Monographs.

Sonnier, K.

Art News. March 1976, p.68.
Pincus-Witten, Robert. 'Keith Sonnier : Video and Film as Colourfield'. *Artforum*. May 1972, pp.35-37.
Smith, Philip. 'Keith Sonnier : Moments in connection'. *Arts*. Nov. 1977, pp.35-37.

Stella, F.

Hopkins, Budd. 'Stella's New Work : A Personal Note'. *Artforum*. Dec. 1976, pp.58-59.
Leder, Philip. 'Stella since 1970'. *Art in America*. March-April, 1978, pp.120-130.
Rosenblum, Robert. *Frank Stella*. London, Penguin, 1971.

Tilson, J.

Gilmour, Pat. 'A Change of He(art) : The Prints of Joe Tilson'. *Print Collector's Newsletter*. Vol.13, No.1, March-April 1982, pp.13-16.
Gilmour, Pat. *Kelpra Studio — The Rose and Chris Prater Gift*. London, Tate Gallery, 1980.

Turner, S.

Turner, S. and Skiold, B. *Handmade Paper Today*. London, Lund Humphries, due 1982.

Tyson, I.

Power, Kevin (ed.). 'Between Poetry and Painting'. *Open Letter*. 4th series, Nos. 1-2, Summer 1978.

Uecker, G.

Judd, Donald. 'Mack-Piene-Uecker. *Arts Magazine*. New York, 1965.
Schmied, W. *Gunther Uecker*. Frankfurt, 1970.

Weege, W.

Print Collector's Newsletter. Vol.12, No.2, May-June 1981, p.49.

Warhol, A.

Tate Gallery, London. *Warhol*. London, The Gallery, 1971. Introduction by Richard Morphet. (Exhibition catalogue).

Zucker, J.

Kertess, Klaus. 'Joe Zucker's Tales of Cotton'. *Arts*. March 1980, pp.161-165.
(10)